THE DISAPPEARING CENTER

ALAN I. ABRAMOWITZ

The Disappearing Center

ENGAGED CITIZENS,
POLARIZATION, AND
AMERICAN DEMOCRACY

YALE UNIVERSITY PRESS   NEW HAVEN & LONDON

Published with assistance from the foundation established
in memory of Philip Hamilton McMillan
of the Class of 1894, Yale College

Set in Scala type by
The Composing Room of Michigan, Inc.
Printed in the United States of America.

Library of Congress Cataloging-in-Publication Data
Abramowitz, Alan I., 1948–
The disappearing center : engaged citizens, polarization, and American
democracy / Alan I. Abramowitz.
p. cm
Includes bibliographical references and index.
ISBN 978-0-300-14162-7 (cloth : alk. paper) 978-0-300-16829-7 (paper)
1. Political parties—United States.   2. Party affiliation—
United States.   3. Polarization (Social sciences)
4. United States—Politics and government—2009–   I. Title.
JK2261.A28   2010
324.273—dc22   2009033737

A catalogue record for this book is available from the British Library.

This paper meets the requirements of ANSI/NISO Z39.48-1992
(Permanence of Paper).

10 9 8 7 6 5 4

For Ann, a model of engaged citizenship

Moderation in temper is always a virtue;
but moderation in principle is always a vice.
Thomas Paine

There's nothing in the middle of the road
but a yellow stripe and dead armadillos.
Jim Hightower

CONTENTS

PREFACE

THE OLD SAYING "BE CAREFUL WHAT YOU wish for, lest it come true" has spe-cial significance for political scientists who study parties and elections in the United States. Back in the 1950s an American Political Science Associ-ation committee made up of some of the leading scholars in the discipline issued a highly critical report on the state of the American two-party sys-tem. That report famously called for the creation of "a more responsible two-party system" in the United States in which programmatic and ideologically cohesive parties would present voters with clear-cut policy choices, and the victorious party would carry out its policy commitments in office. It was a prescription that seemed rather far-fetched given the lack of ideological co-hesion of the two major parties at the time. The report also quickly drew fire from defenders of the status quo who saw important advantages to non-programmatic, ideologically diverse parties and policy making based on bi-partisan compromise.

Fifty years later, many of the goals of the APSA committee have become reality, owing not to any reforms instituted in response to the report itself but to the strategic behavior of office-seeking politicians and the changing characteristics of the American electorate. Today American voters choose between ideologically cohesive parties with sharply contrasting positions on many of the leading issues of the day. But many students of American pol-itics are not convinced that the country is better off as a result of these developments. Some bemoan the decline of bipartisanship in Washington, and others see a growing disconnect between a polarized elite and a public that remains largely moderate.

The central argument of this volume is that there is no disconnect between the political elite and the American people. Polarization in Washington reflects polarization within the public, especially within the politically engaged segment of the public. It is the politically engaged segment of the public—the attentive, informed, and active citizens—that most closely reflects the ideals of democratic citizenship, and it is the politically engaged segment of the public that is the most partisan and ideologically polarized. In contrast, it is among the least attentive, least informed, and least active members of the public that partisanship is weakest and moderation thrives.

Far from turning Americans off on politics, polarization has served to energize the public by clarifying the stakes in elections. Voter turnout increased dramatically in 2004 and reached its highest level in more than four decades in 2008. In 2008 more Americans than ever voted in primary elections, talked to their friends and neighbors about the election, gave money to parties and candidates, and displayed yard signs and bumper stickers. Today the engaged public is larger than ever before and that can only be a good thing for American democracy.

I owe a debt of gratitude to many individuals whose ideas have contributed to my thinking about polarization and American democracy. I have benefited greatly from my collaboration with Kyle Saunders of Colorado State University, Ronald Rapoport of the College of William and Mary, Walter Stone of the University of California at Davis, and Ruy Teixeira of the Center for American Progress. Larry Sabato of the Center for Politics at the University of Virginia and Bill Bishop of the *Austin American-Statesman* have influenced my thinking about recent trends in American society and politics. And I am grateful to Jim Campbell of the State University of New York at Buffalo for providing a useful perspective on polarization from the other side of the partisan and ideological divide. I have also learned much from my colleagues at Emory University including Merle Black, Randall Strahan, Thomas Remington, and Micheal Giles. I would also like to thank my editor at the Yale University Press, William Frucht, for his encouragement on this project and for stimulating my thinking about the causes and consequences of polarization. Finally, I would like to thank my wife, Ann, for her encouragement and support on this project and for providing a shining example of the benefits of engaged citizenship.

Polarization in the Age of Obama

ON NOVEMBER 2, 2004, AMERICANS went to the polls after one of the most divisive election campaigns in modern history. Just more than three years after the terrorist attacks of September 11, 2001, had united the country and earned President George W. Bush an approval rating of close to 90 percent, the nation found itself deeply divided over such issues as abortion, gay marriage, and above all, the president's conduct of the war in Iraq. Public opinion polls showed that the electorate was almost evenly split between those who strongly supported the president and his policies and those who strongly opposed him and his policies. Very few voters were ambivalent.

The result of the 2004 election was a relatively narrow reelection victory for Bush, who captured 50.7 percent of the popular vote and 286 electoral votes, versus 48.3 percent of the popular vote and 252 electoral votes for his Democratic challenger, Massachusetts senator John Kerry.[1] But even after the president's victory, the nation remained as divided as ever. Bush made little effort to reach out to Kerry or his supporters, and Democratic leaders in Congress, after offering perfunctory words of congratulation, promised to vigorously oppose the president's agenda.[2]

To many political observers, the intense divisions within the country over President Bush and his policies, along with the inability of Democrats and Republicans in Congress to work together on major issues, were indicators of a fundamental problem with American politics in the twenty-first century. That problem was polarization. According to these observers, the sharp divisions between Democratic and Republican leaders were driving a wedge between party supporters in the electorate and alienating many moderate citizens from the political process.[3]

There is no question that policy differences between Democrats and Republicans in Washington have increased over the past several decades. Conservative Democrats and liberal Republicans who once occupied key leadership positions in the House and Senate have almost disappeared, and there are far fewer moderates in both parties. The sharp divisions evident in the 2004 presidential election were the result of a long-term trend toward ideologically polarized political parties—a trend that has made bipartisan cooperation and compromise much more difficult.[4]

Polarization did not begin with George W. Bush, who was a product of a party system that was already characterized by a high degree of polarization. The roots of that polarization can be traced back to the southern strategy of Richard Nixon, the courtship of conservative Democrats by Ronald Reagan, the takeover of the Republican Party in Congress by southern conservatives led by Newt Gingrich, and the divisive battle over the impeachment of President Bill Clinton. And polarization is unlikely to go away with the departure of Bush from Washington in early 2009.

During the 2008 presidential campaign, Democratic senator Barack Obama promised, if elected, to change the tone in the nation's capital by reaching out to Republicans and including them in the policy-making process. And indeed, during his first days in office, Obama did reach out to Republicans—inviting three of them to join his cabinet and traveling to the House and Senate to meet with Republican members and urge them to support his economic stimulus package. In an attempt to win more Republican votes, the president even agreed to include larger tax cuts and smaller spending increases in his proposal than his economic advisors were recommending. In the end, though, the ideological chasm between the parties was simply too wide to bridge. Not one Republican voted for the stimulus bill in the House of Representatives. In the Senate, only three moderate northeastern Republicans, the last survivors of a dying breed, voted for the bill—one more than was needed to avert a filibuster.

The deep partisan divide in Congress on this issue was reflected by a comparable divide in the public. A Gallup Poll conducted February 8–10, just be-

fore the House and Senate voted on the final version of the stimulus legislation, showed that the president's plan was supported by 82 percent of
Democrats but only 28 percent of Republicans. This 54-point gap was similar in magnitude to that found on such divisive issues as the war in Iraq during the Bush years.

In the aftermath of the stimulus debate, a Fox News Poll on February 17–
18 found a sharp difference in how Democrats and Republicans evaluated
Obama's performance. Although the president's overall approval rating was
a very respectable 60 percent, about twice that of his predecessor during his
final days in office, his approval rating was only 29 percent among Republicans compared with 90 percent among Democrats. After Obama had been
in office for only four weeks, the 61-point partisan gap in evaluations of him
was almost as large as the partisan gap in evaluations of President Bush
during most of his second term.

Despite his oft-repeated promise to change the tone in Washington and
his efforts to reach out to Republicans, Barack Obama, during his first few
weeks in the White House, was having little success in overcoming the reality of ideological polarization in both Washington and the nation. But is polarization entirely a bad thing for American democracy? After all, a record
123 million Americans went to the polls in the 2004 presidential election,
an increase of some 18 million over 2000. In 2008, that number increased
by another 9 million, to 132 million. The estimated turnout of eligible voters rose from 55 percent in 2000 to 60 percent in 2004 and 62 percent in
2008, which was the highest in decades and close to the levels seen during
the peak turnout years of the 1960s before eighteen-to-twenty-year-olds were
added to the electorate. Turnout increased among every major subgroup
within the electorate, including African Americans, Hispanics, and those
younger than thirty.[5]

And Americans weren't just voting in record numbers. According to data
from the American National Election Studies (ANES), they were also talking
to their friends and neighbors about the election, displaying yard signs and
bumper stickers, and donating money to the parties and candidates in
record numbers. The evidence from the 2004 and 2008 presidential elections indicates that although some Americans may have been turned off by
polarization, many others were energized by it.

The thesis of this book is that American politics has become more polarized in recent years and that this development has had both positive and negative consequences for democracy. I argue that the key to understanding polarization in the United States and its consequences for democracy is the role played by a group that I call the *engaged public.* This group is made up of citizens who care about government and politics, pay attention to what political leaders are saying and doing, and participate actively in the political process. The engaged public plays a critical role in American politics because its members make up the electoral bases of the Democratic and Republican parties. Officeholders and candidates cultivate their support because they are a crucial source of campaign contributions and volunteer labor, they constitute the bulk of the voters in most primary elections, and they provide a large proportion of the votes needed to win general elections. In many states and congressional districts dominated by one party, the support of engaged partisans may be enough to ensure a candidate's reelection.

The size and partisan composition of the engaged public can vary over time depending on the national political climate and the electoral cycle. Thus, the engaged public can expand during a presidential campaign that features sharp differences over highly charged issues, such as the 2004 Bush-Kerry campaign. The partisan balance can also be affected by the national political climate. During the 2006 and 2008 election campaigns, for example, some evidence shows that Democrats were more energized than Republicans.[6] In general, though, the partisan balance among the engaged public in recent years has reflected the close partisan balance within the overall electorate.

Political engagement is a continuous variable rather than a simple dichotomy. Americans possess widely varying levels of involvement in the political process. Few are totally apolitical and few are political junkies whose lives revolve around government and politics. Nevertheless, during any time period it is possible to distinguish those who are generally interested, informed, and active from those who are generally uninterested, uninformed, and inactive.

Three major arguments about the engaged public and American democracy run through this book. The first is that partisan-ideological polarization is greatest among those individuals whose beliefs and behavior most closely reflect the ideals of responsible democratic citizenship, that is, the engaged public. In contrast, partisan-ideological polarization is lowest among those individuals whose beliefs and behavior are the farthest removed from the ideals of responsible democratic citizenship, that is, the politically disengaged. It is among the uninterested, uninformed, and inactive that ideological moderation and independence flourish.

The second major argument is that there is no disconnect between political elites and the public. However, candidates and elected officials pay disproportionate attention to the views of the politically engaged segment of the public, which is also the most ideologically polarized segment of the public. Therefore, polarization at the elite level is largely a reflection of polarization among the politically engaged segment of the American public.

The third major argument is that by clarifying choices and increasing the stakes in elections, partisan-ideological polarization can increase the interest and motivation of members of the public to vote and engage in other political activities, thereby increasing the size of the engaged public. As a result of increasing polarization as well as increasing mobilization efforts by parties, candidates, and other organizations, politically engaged citizens made up a larger share of the public during the 2004 and 2008 presidential campaigns than at any time in recent history. This development was reflected not only in higher voter turnout, but also in increased participation in other political activities such as talking about politics with friends and neighbors, displaying yard signs and bumper stickers, and giving money to political parties and candidates. At the same time, despite or perhaps because of growing partisan polarization, a large segment of the American public remained uninterested and uninvolved in the political process. For those who do not understand or care about the partisan and ideological divisions that dominate contemporary political discourse, the polarization evident in the 2004 and 2008 presidential campaigns may have been more of a turn off than a turn on.

There is another potential problem with growing partisan-ideological polarization. As ideological differences between the two major parties have increased and ideological differences within each party have diminished, electoral competition in the United States has come to closely resemble the British model of responsible party government: voters now have a choice in presidential and congressional elections between unified party teams offering clear-cut policy alternatives. The problem is that American political institutions were not designed with responsible party government in mind.

Responsible party government requires strongly majoritarian political institutions that allow the winning party team to implement the policies chosen by the voters.[7] But the American political system includes a number of important antimajoritarian features such as lifetime appointment of federal judges, overrepresentation of small states in the Senate and the Electoral College, the presidential veto, and the Senate filibuster. In addition, the potential for divided government can create confusion about who has the right to implement the will of the majority—the president or the majority party in Congress.

These features of the American political system can make it difficult for the winning party team to implement its policy proposals, as the victorious Democrats discovered in the aftermath of their takeover of Congress in the 2006 midterm elections. Without sixty votes in the Senate to cut off debate or two-thirds majorities in the House and Senate to override presidential vetoes, congressional Democrats were unable to enact many of the policies on which they campaigned in 2006, including a swift end to the war in Iraq. The result was frustration among a large segment of the public, including many Democrats who expected their party's victory to produce dramatic changes in public policy.[8]

The Plan of This Book

Chapter 2 examines the size and characteristics of the engaged public in the United States. I present evidence concerning trends and variations in political engagement in the American public over time using evidence from the ANES concerning interest in politics, awareness of party positions, and participation in the electoral process. I show that political engagement among the public reached its highest level in 2008, and I present evidence that this was a direct result of the deep divisions within the public over the presidency of George W. Bush. Finally, I argue that the primary explanation for these deep divisions was the high level of partisan-ideological polarization among the politically engaged segment of the public and that this is unlikely to change under a new president.

Chapter 3 examines the meaning and measurement of polarization in the American public and presents evidence of growing polarization, especially among the politically engaged. Many political analysts and scholars have discussed polarization in the United States, but few have actually tried to define it. I argue that polarization has two components: it is important to specify both *what* the public is polarized about and *who* is polarized. Some citizens may be primarily concerned with one issue or a limited set of issues. In recent years, for instance, a great deal of attention has been focused on polarization over cultural issues such as abortion and gay marriage. More recently, scholars have examined polarization over the war in Iraq. However, I argue that it is more useful to conceptualize polarization in terms of consistency across a *variety* of issues, including cultural issues, economic and social welfare issues, and national security issues. The more consistent citizens' opinions are across a range of issues, the stronger their preferences will be with regard to political parties, candidates, and officeholders.

I argue that party leaders and elected officials are an important source of cues for citizens with regard to policy issues and therefore an important source of polarization among the politically attentive segment of the public. As party leaders and elected officials have become increasingly consistent in their views across a variety of issues, the public, and especially the politically attentive segment of the public, has followed suit. Politically engaged partisans now display more consistent views across a range of issues than in the past, with Democratic identifiers increasingly clustered on the left side of the ideological spectrum and Republican identifiers on the right. As a result, partisanship and ideology have become much more closely related, and the overall distribution of ideological preferences among the public, and especially among the politically engaged, has shifted from a unimodal distribution toward a bimodal distribution, with Democrats on the left and Republicans on the right. Although the process of partisan-ideological polarization may have been initiated by political elites, growing polarization among politically engaged citizens means that the behavior of candidates and elected officials is increasingly constrained by the preferences of their most active and informed supporters.

Chapter 4 examines how partisan-ideological realignment has shaped the party loyalties of major social groups in the United States. Over the past half century the American party system has been transformed from one based primarily on group loyalties forged during the New Deal and earlier to one based primarily on ideology. Some social cleavages, particularly those based on region, social class, and religious affiliation, have been diminishing in importance since the 1960s as a result of this ideological realignment. At the same time, however, differences based on gender, martial status, and above all, religious commitment have been increasing. The growing religious divide in American politics reflects the increasing prominence of cultural issues such as abortion, gay rights, and stem cell research in national politics and the increasing association of the two major parties with opposing positions on these issues.

Over the past forty years, the traditional alignment of white Catholic voters with the Democratic Party and white mainstream Protestant voters outside of the South with the Republican Party has been diminishing. Religious conservatives of all faiths have been shifting their allegiance toward the Republican Party while religious moderates and secular voters have been shifting their allegiance toward the Democratic Party; these shifts have been most dramatic among the politically engaged segment of the public. As a result, among white voters today the religious divide is much deeper than the class divide. In the 2004 and 2008 presidential elections, as well as in the 2006 midterm elections, the large majority of lower income whites who attended religious services regularly voted for Republican candidates while a majority of upper income whites who rarely or never attended religious services voted for Democratic candidates.

There is one important exception to the general rule that party loyalties today are based mainly on ideology rather than group identity. That exception is race. Politically engaged black Americans tend to have more liberal views on most issues and are much less likely to identify themselves as conservatives than white Americans. However, regardless of their views on specific issues or their ideological identification, black Americans, and especially politically engaged black Americans, overwhelmingly identify with the Democratic Party. This has been true since the 1960s when Democratic president Lyndon Johnson embraced the cause of civil rights and the Republican Party began to aggressively court the southern white vote. Recent efforts by Republican candidates and officeholders to make inroads among black voters by appealing to the conservative sentiments of religious blacks on social issues or opposition to higher taxes and public spending among more affluent blacks have thus far met with very limited success. In contrast to every other major social group in the United States, black Americans remain almost monolithic in their support for the Democratic Party, and the candidacy of Barack Obama in 2008 only reinforced this loyalty. According to the 2008 National Exit Poll, a remarkable 95 percent of African American voters supported the Democratic nominee.

Chapter 5 examines the consequences of the growing partisan-ideological divide in American politics for the electoral process. I show that this trend has had important consequences for voting behavior and electoral competition, resulting in a substantial increase in party line voting and a substantial decrease in ticket splitting. Voters today are much less likely to defect from their party in presidential or congressional elections than in the past because their partisan and ideological orientations are more consistent than in the past.

Since the 1970s the number and population of states in which one party or the other enjoys a dominant position has increased dramatically; concomitantly, the number of swing states has decreased. A similar trend can be seen at the county level and in the nation's congressional districts. Although the two major parties remain highly competitive at the national level, a fact reflected by the results of recent presidential elections, competition at the subnational level has declined markedly as a result of growing one-party dominance in many constituencies and increased partisan consistency in voting behavior.

Contrary to what appears to be a widely held belief among pundits and media commentators, the decline in the number of competitive congressional districts, like the decline in the number of competitive states and counties, cannot be explained by partisan gerrymandering. Instead, it is a product of an ideological realignment that has produced a dramatic increase in the correspondence between ideology and partisanship among the engaged public. The movement of conservative whites in the South from the Democratic Party to the Republican Party has been perhaps the most obvious manifestation of this trend. Less noticed but equally significant has been the movement of moderate-to-liberal whites in the metropolitan areas of the

Northeast, Midwest, and Pacific Coast from the Republican Party to the Democratic Party.[9]

Migration patterns have reinforced the effects of this ideological realignment. Americans, especially relatively affluent, college-educated Americans, are increasingly choosing where to live on the basis of lifestyle preferences that are strongly related to political attitudes. Younger, unmarried individuals who tend to have liberal political attitudes generally cluster in the larger cities and their inner suburbs while married couples with children who tend to have more conservative political attitudes generally cluster in the outer suburbs. This trend has been described by Bill Bishop as "the big sort" and by Ronald Brownstein as "the great sorting out."[10] Over the past thirty years, the percentage of Americans living in counties dominated by one party has increased dramatically while the percentage living in counties that are politically competitive has decreased dramatically. Americans are increasingly surrounded by those who share their political outlook: liberal Democrats by other liberal Democrats, and conservative Republicans by other conservative Republicans.

The growing number of states and congressional districts in which one party enjoys a dominant position, along with increased partisan consistency in voting behavior, have made it much more difficult today for a candidate from the minority party to win a House or Senate contest. Election outcomes increasingly reflect the partisan composition of the electorate in a state or congressional district.

The growing partisan-ideological divide has also had important consequences for political campaigns. Growing consistency between partisanship and ideology has made it much more difficult for candidates to appeal for support across party lines. As a result, campaigns have become more focused on mobilizing co-partisans and less focused on persuading swing voters or opposing partisans. Because of the close division between Democrats and Republicans in the national electorate and the winner-take-all rule followed by almost all states in awarding electoral votes, presidential campaigns tend to focus on a relatively small number of swing states. Even in these swing states, however, the campaigns have become increasingly concerned with mobilizing their core supporters.

Finally, growing partisan-ideological polarization has had important consequences for primary campaigns and elections. Over the past several decades, ideological differences between Democratic and Republican voters have increased while ideological differences among voters within each party have decreased. Growing ideological homogeneity within both major parties has contributed to a decline in primary competition, especially in races involving incumbents. In the absence of a scandal or some other personal problem, an incumbent whose policy positions fall within the ideological mainstream of his or her party is unlikely to experience a serious primary challenge. Even in nomination contests without an incumbent, such as the 2008 Democratic and Republican presidential races, policy differences among primary candidates are generally minimal. As a result, primary voters tend to choose candidates on the basis of their personal qualities or perceived electability.

Chapter 6 focuses on how the trends documented in the previous chapters are likely to play out in the future. How will the departure of George W. Bush from the political scene affect partisan conflict and electoral competition? Will one of the legacies of his presidency be an extended period of deepening partisanship and conflict, or will partisan-ideological polarization diminish as new political leaders take center stage?

The conduct of the candidates seeking the 2008 Democratic and Republican presidential nominations and the general election contest between Barack Obama and John McCain indicate that we are likely to witness a continuation and perhaps even a deepening of partisan-ideological polarization in the near future. An observer following the 2008 presidential nomination campaigns might well have concluded that the Democratic and Republican candidates were running for the presidencies of two different countries. On the Democratic side, all of the major candidates, including Obama, favored rapidly withdrawing U.S. military forces from Iraq, stepping up diplomatic efforts to ease tensions with Iran, ending tax breaks on the wealthiest Americans, and expanding the role of the federal government in providing health insurance and protecting the environment. On the Republican side, all of the leading candidates, including McCain, favored continuing the U.S. military presence in Iraq, using the threat of air strikes to force Iran to end its nuclear program, making the Bush tax cuts permanent, and relying on free market incentives to increase health-care coverage and protect the environment. The overall picture presented by the 2008 presidential campaign was one of intense partisan polarization, with relatively minor policy differences among the candidates within each party along with sharp policy differences between the two parties.

Given the evidence presented in this book, it is hardly surprising that all of the major candidates seeking the Democratic and Republican presidential nominations took sharply contrasting positions on a wide range of domestic and foreign policy issues. These positions appear to accurately reflect the views of politically engaged supporters of the two parties. Moreover, given the polarized views of the two parties' engaged supporters, it is not surprising that neither Barack Obama nor John McCain showed much evidence of moderating his positions on major issues during the general election campaign in order to appeal to swing voters. Any such move toward the center clearly would have risked alienating a large proportion of the party's electoral base. In fact, the most dramatic action that either candidate took during the campaign may have been McCain's choice of Alaska governor Sarah Palin as his running mate—a choice clearly designed to energize the conservative base of the Republican Party, not to appeal to moderate and independent swing voters.

Even though George Bush was not on the ballot, the 2008 presidential campaign was just as bruising and divisive as the 2004 campaign. But it was also exciting and energizing. With the two parties presenting the electorate with clear choices on issues ranging from the economy and health care to the war in Iraq and global warming, the level of public engagement in the 2008 campaign was even higher than that in 2004.[11] From the beginning of the nomination campaign, Democratic voters were especially enthusiastic about voting, turning out in record numbers for their party's presidential primaries.[12] In November almost 132 million Americans voted in the presidential election, an increase of some 9 million over 2004. The 62 percent turnout rate of eligible voters was the highest in forty years.

In addition to examining polarization in the 2008 election, Chapter 6 considers how partisan-ideological polarization may interact with long-term demographic trends, such as rising education levels and the declining proportion of married white Christians in the population, to shape the American electorate in the future. These trends suggest that there is a potential for continued growth in political engagement within the electorate along with a gradual shift in the balance of party identification in favor of the Democratic Party. Indeed, recent polling data suggest that this shift has been going on for several years and played a major role in Obama's victory in the 2008 presidential election.

Chapter 7 examines the consequences of growing partisan-ideological polarization for representation in Congress. Over the past three decades, ideological differences between Democrats and Republicans in Congress have increased dramatically. Today, very few conservative Democrats or liberal Republicans are left in either the House of Representatives or the Senate. According to many journalists and reform advocates, partisan redistricting is largely responsible for this development: partisan gerrymandering has resulted in more safe districts and fewer marginal districts, thereby decreasing the need for members of Congress to take moderate positions in order to appeal to swing voters. However, the evidence presented in this chapter does not support this hypothesis. Redistricting has not been a major factor in the decline of marginal districts since the 1970s. Moreover, ideological polarization has increased among representatives from marginal as well as safe districts and among senators as well as representatives. In the 108th Congress, representatives from marginal districts were almost as polarized as representatives from safe districts. An alternative explanation for increasing ideological polarization in Congress is increasing ideological polarization among Democratic and Republican voters. This trend helps to explain the high levels of party unity evident in both the Senate and House of Representatives in recent years and the difficulty of building bipartisan coalitions on legislation.

In the concluding chapter I discuss the consequences of growing partisan-ideological polarization for American democracy in the twenty-first century. This chapter considers the implications of partisan-ideological polarization for two fundamental issues in democratic politics: popular participation and elite responsiveness. From the standpoint of popular participation, the key question is how increasing polarization affects the level of political engagement in the mass public. Here the evidence is quite clear: although a small proportion of Americans may be turned off by polarization, a much larger proportion are energized by it. By providing voters with a clear choice between parties representing divergent policy alternatives, polarization increases interest and participation in the electoral process among the public.

From the standpoint of elite responsiveness, the key question is how the growing partisan-ideological divide among political elites and the engaged segment of the public will interact with political institutions that can make it difficult for the winning party team to carry out its policy commitments. Despite the nostalgia of some political commentators for a lost era of bipartisan consensus, the traditional bipartisan approach in which public policy is based on compromise between key leaders in both major parties now appears to be almost dead. The differences between the parties are too great and the numbers of moderates in both parties are too small to permit such bipartisan agreements on major policy issues. The question is, what will replace the politics of bipartisan compromise? I argue that the only realistic alternative to continued gridlock in Washington is not a revival of bipartisanship, but an American version of responsible party government in which one party enjoys simultaneous control of the executive and legislative branches with enough votes to overcome filibuster threats in the Senate.

The results of the 2008 presidential and congressional elections may provide a test of whether this American form of responsible party government can work.

2

The Engaged Public

STUDENTS OF PUBLIC OPINION OFTEN describe ordinary Americans as uninterested in politics, uninformed about political issues, and uninvolved in the political process beyond occasionally voting in national elections.[1] In his seminal study "The Nature of Belief Systems in Mass Publics," Philip Converse analyzed data from the 1956 and 1960 ANES surveys and concluded that the large majority of Americans lacked any coherent ideological perspective on politics and that many did not even have meaningful opinions on the leading issues of the day. Converse argued that the kind of ideological thinking prevalent among political leaders was confined to a tiny minority of educated and informed citizens.[2]

To a considerable extent, Converse's characterization of the public as uninterested, uninformed, and unsophisticated remains the conventional wisdom among students of American public opinion in the twenty-first century. Thus, in his popular and influential book *Culture War? The Myth of a Polarized America*, Morris Fiorina concludes that Converse's portrait of the American public "still holds up pretty well." According to Fiorina, the ideological disputes that engage political elites and party activists have little resonance among the American mass public: like their mid-twentieth-century counterparts, ordinary twenty-first-century Americans "are not very well-informed about politics, do not hold many of their views very strongly, and are not ideological."[3]

The central argument of this chapter is that this portrait of the American public as generally apathetic with regard to politics is fundamentally flawed. In the first place, sweeping generalizations about the political beliefs and behavior of ordinary Americans ignore the fact that there are vast differences in political interest, knowledge, and activity among the public. Although some Americans have little interest in government and politics, know very little about political leaders or current issues, and rarely participate in politics beyond occasionally voting, many ordinary Americans care deeply about political issues, follow news about government and politics closely, and not only vote but discuss politics with their friends and relatives, display yard signs and bumper stickers during campaigns, and donate money to parties and candidates. Any analysis of the political beliefs and behavior of the American public must take these differences in political engagement into account.

Along with the fact that ordinary Americans display a wide range of political interest, knowledge, and activity, evidence from recent surveys of the electorate shows that today the engaged public is quite large. One indicator of political engagement is interest in and concern about the results of elections, and in 2004, 84 percent of respondents in the ANES preelection survey indicated that they were at least somewhat interested in the political campaigns and 40 percent indicated that they were very interested. The level of interest was even higher in the postelection wave: 91 percent of respondents indicated that they were at least somewhat interested, and 51 percent were very interested. In the same survey, 85 percent of respondents in the preelection wave said that they cared "a good deal" about who won the presidential election, and 67 percent were "very much" or "pretty much" concerned about which party won the elections to the U.S. House of Representatives.

Political information provides a somewhat more demanding test of the public's engagement in the political process than mere interest. Here, the evidence from the 2004 ANES is limited. However, one piece of evidence that is available shows that a substantial majority of survey respondents were aware of the ideological positions of the two major parties and presidential candidates. When asked to place the parties and candidates on a 7-point liberal-conservative scale, 60 percent of respondents placed the Democratic Party on the liberal side of the scale, and 65 percent placed the Republican

Party on the conservative side. Only 14 percent of respondents placed the Democratic Party on the conservative side, and only 15 percent placed the Republican Party on the liberal side. Similarly, 59 percent of respondents placed the Democratic presidential candidate, John Kerry, on the liberal side of the scale, and 63 percent placed the Republican candidate, George Bush, on the conservative side. Only 13 percent placed Kerry on the conservative side, and only 17 percent placed Bush on the liberal side.

When we compare respondents' placements of the two major parties and the two presidential candidates, we find that 64 percent placed the Democratic Party to the left of the Republican Party and 62 percent placed Kerry to the left of Bush. Only 12 percent of respondents placed the Democratic Party to the right of the Republican Party, and only 12 percent placed Kerry to the right of Bush.

The data from the 2004 ANES indicate that the majority of Americans were able to accurately distinguish the ideological positions of the two major parties and presidential candidates in 2004. Moreover, the accuracy of these ideological placements increases when we focus on those respondents who reported voting in the election. Among these self-identified voters, 71 percent placed the Democratic Party to the left of the Republican Party, and 70 percent placed Kerry to the left of Bush. Only 11 percent of self-identified voters placed the Democratic Party to the right of the Republican Party, and only 11 percent placed Kerry to the right of Bush.

Our final and perhaps most important indicator of political engagement is participation in the political process. Here, the evidence from the 2004 ANES indicates that while only a small minority of respondents could be described as political activists, many reported not only voting in the presidential election, but engaging in political activities beyond voting, such as trying to persuade a friend or neighbor to vote for their candidate, displaying a bumper sticker or yard sign for a candidate, contributing money to a party or candidate, attending a campaign meeting or rally, or working on a campaign. The data displayed in Figure 2.1 show that 85 percent reported engaging in at least one campaign-related activity, more than half in at least two activities, and about a quarter in at least three activities. Almost two-thirds of those who reported voting indicated that they had engaged in at least one additional campaign-related activity.

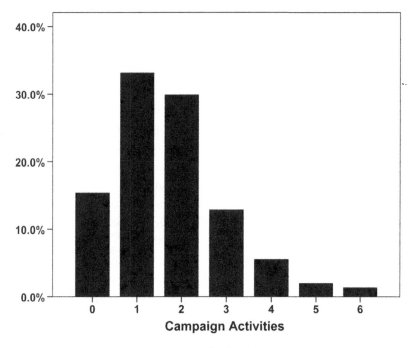

Figure 2.1. Campaign-related activities in 2004.
(*Source:* 2004 American National Election Study.)

In recent years a number of pundits and political commentators have claimed that ordinary Americans are turned off by the hyperpartisanship and polarization that they see in Washington. In their view, most Americans have little interest in the ideological battles that preoccupy the politicians and their activist supporters, and they have become increasingly frustrated that Democrats and Republicans are unable or unwilling to work together to address the major problems facing the country. As a result, we are told, ordinary Americans are losing faith in the political process. But the evidence from the 2004 ANES casts serious doubt on this argument. Even allowing for the tendency of survey respondents to exaggerate their political activities, these results indicate that there was a fairly high level of involvement in the 2004 campaign among the American public. Moreover, evidence from the ANES time series shows that the level of political engagement among the public has been increasing.

Contrary to the claim that ordinary Americans have been losing interest in government and politics as a result of growing partisan animosity and ideological polarization, the evidence displayed in Table 2.1, based on questions that have been included in ANES surveys since the 1960s, shows that Americans today are more interested in politics, better informed about public affairs, and more politically active than at any time during the past half century. On every one of these measures, including interviewers' assessments of the respondents' level of political information, Americans during the first decade of the twenty-first century scored higher than their counterparts in the 1960s, 1970s, 1980s, and 1990s. On every one of these measures, political engagement increased by between 10 and 22 percentage points from the 1980s to the 2000s.

On a number of measures, including the percentage of respondents stating that they cared a good deal about who won the presidential election and

Table 2.1. Indicators of political engagement by decade

	1962–1970 (%)	1972–1980 (%)	1982–1990 (%o	1992–2000 (%o	2002–2004 (%)	Change 1980s–2000s (%)
Very or somewhat interested in election	75	73	71	77	81	+10
Follow public affairs most or some of the time	67	67	62	64	73	+11
Care which party wins presidency	65	58	63	77	85	+22
Care which party wins Congress	62	50	52	60	71	+19
Information rated very or fairly high	38	34	36	43	57	+21
Politically active beyond voting	33	31	27	32	43	+16

Source: American National Election Study Cumulative File.

the percentage who reported trying to persuade a friend or relative to vote for a candidate, the level of political engagement in the American public in 2004 was the highest in the history of the ANES. And it appears that political engagement in the American public was even higher in 2008. The 2008 presidential election sparked the interest of the American people like no other in the past forty years, from the first caucuses and primaries in January all the way until Election Day. In a January 2008 Washington Post/ABC News Poll, 79 percent of Americans reported that they were following the presidential campaign at least somewhat closely; 32 percent stated that they were following the campaign very closely. In January 2004, only 66 percent of Americans were following the presidential campaign at least somewhat closely, and only 22 percent were following it very closely; and in January 2000 only 50 percent of Americans were following the presidential campaign at least somewhat closely and only 11 percent very closely.

Gallup Poll data show a similar trend. In a survey conducted January 10–13, 2008, 64 percent of respondents stated that they had given "quite a lot" of thought to the upcoming presidential election. This was the highest level ever recorded in a Gallup Poll in January of a presidential election year. By comparison, the proportion of respondents who claimed that they had given "quite a lot" of thought to the presidential election was only 48 percent in January 2004 and only 32 percent in January 2000.[4]

Voter turnout in 2008 reflected the extraordinary level of interest measured by the polls. Almost 60 million voters participated in the presidential primaries and caucuses, far more than in any previous election. Participation in Democratic primaries and caucuses more than doubled, from around 17 million in 2004 to around 37 million in 2008. Close to 132 million voters cast ballots in the November election, an increase of 9 million over the 2004 figure of 123 million. The estimated turnout of 62 percent of eligible voters was one of the highest since World War II and the highest since the vote was extended to eighteen-to-twenty-year-olds in 1972.

Measuring Political Engagement

All of the variables included in Table 2.1—interest in politics and public affairs, concern about the results of presidential and congressional elections, political information, and political participation—are closely related. This can be seen in Table 2.2, which displays the correlations (Pearson *r*) among these six items in the ANES time series. The correlations range from .25 to .51 and are all highly statistically significant. This suggests that all of these items are measuring different aspects of a common underlying trait: political engagement. Therefore, in order to measure the overall level of political engagement in the American public, I combined these six items into a scale. The scale has a reliability coefficient (Cronbach α) of .75. (A coefficient of .7 or greater is generally considered satisfactory.) Scores on this scale range from 0 for the least politically engaged respondents to 13 for the most politically engaged respondents.

The six variables included in the political engagement scale were all included in only five ANES surveys—those conducted in 1980, 1992, 1996, 2000, and 2004. As a result, we can compare scores on the scale for only these five years. Fortunately, this gives us a long enough time span to determine whether there has been any trend in the overall level of political engagement in the American public.

Figure 2.2 displays the trend in the mean score of ANES respondents on the political engagement scale between 1980 and 2004. The results shown in Figure 2.2 indicate that political engagement in the American public increased substantially between 1980 and 1992, declined modestly between 1992 and 1996, increased slightly between 1996 and 2000, and again increased substantially between 2000 and 2004. By the end of this period, which coincided with a dramatic rise in partisan-ideological polarization among political elites, the overall level of political engagement in the public was considerably higher than it had been at the beginning. These results suggest that growing partisan-ideological polarization among political elites, rather than turning ordinary Americans off on politics, may have contributed to an increase in the size of the engaged public.

Explaining Variation in Political Engagement

Of course, even after the increase in political engagement evident in Figure 2.2, dramatic differences in political engagement remain among the American public. Many Americans were caught up in the excitement of the

Table 2.2. Correlations among indicators of political engagement

	Public affairs	Care, president	Care, Congress	Info rating	Political activity
Election interest	.51	.41	.37	.42	.44
Public affairs	—	.25	.41	.46	.40
Care, president	—	—	.32	.28	.29
Care, Congress	—	—	—	.29	.36
Info rating	—	—	—	—	.40

Source: American National Election Study Cumulative File.
Note: Coefficients shown are Pearson product-moment correlations. All coefficients are significant at the .001 level.

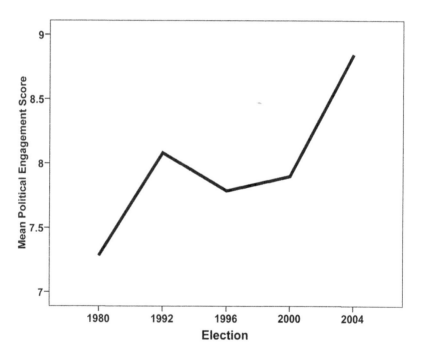

Figure 2.2. Trends in political engagement, 1980–2004.
(*Source:* American National Election Studies.)

2004 and 2008 presidential elections, but many others chose to stay on the sidelines, focusing instead on such things as the activities of Hollywood celebrities, their favorite sports teams, or the daily struggle to raise their families and make ends meet. Political involvement requires time, re-sources, and motivation, and these are unevenly distributed among the public.

Political scientists have identified a number of social characteristics that affect Americans' involvement in the political process, including age, edu-cation, income, gender, and race.[5] These characteristics can influence both the cost of obtaining political information and the rewards that individuals receive from following and participating in the political process.[6] In gen-eral, older, better educated, and more affluent Americans tend to be more politically interested, knowledgeable, and active than younger, less educated, and less affluent Americans. Traditionally, women and nonwhites have also been less involved in the political process than men and whites, largely be-cause they were excluded from actively participating in politics until fairly re-cently. However, as the legal and extralegal barriers to participation by women and nonwhites have been removed, these differences have dimin-ished.[7] In addition, two other characteristics—partisanship and ideology—may be important motivations for political involvement today. As partisan-ideological polarization among political elites has increased, individuals with strong partisan and ideological preferences should perceive greater stakes in the political process than individuals with weaker partisan and ideological preferences.

The evidence displayed in Table 2.3 indicates that all of the characteristics discussed above were related to political engagement in 2004. Older Amer-icans were more likely to score high on political engagement than younger Americans, college graduates were much more likely to score high than those with only a high school education, and individuals with higher in-comes were much more likely to score high than those with lower incomes. Even though some of the barriers to participation in the political process by women and nonwhites have been removed, these groups still scored some-what lower on political engagement than men and whites. Finally, strong partisans scored much higher than weak partisans and independents, and strong liberals and conservatives (those with scores of 1, 2, 6, or 7 on the

Table 2.3. Political engagement of subgroups in 2004

	% Highly engaged	(n of cases)
Age		
18–29	23	(202)
30–39	28	(165)
40–49	38	(192)
50–64	42	(293)
65+	38	(183)
Education		
High school or less	20	(389)
Some college	32	(334)
Graduated college	56	(312)
Family income		
Lower third	23	(343)
Middle third	38	(288)
Upper third	51	(289)
Gender		
Male	39	(492)
Female	31	(543)
Race		
White	39	(739)
Black	24	(157)
Other	28	(134)
Partisan intensity		
Pure independent	13	(97)
Leaning or weak	28	(580)
Strong	54	(344)
Ideological intensity		
None, moderate	20	(457)
Lean liberal or conservative	36	(262)
Strong liberal or conservative	56	(314)

Source: 2004 American National Election Study.

7-point liberal-conservative scale) scored much higher than moderates or individuals with only a weak ideological preference.

In order to compare the effects of all of these variables on political engagement in 2004, I performed a multiple regression analysis with the political engagement scale as the dependent variable. Table 2.4 shows the results of this regression analysis. I have reported the beta weights, or standardized regression coefficients, for each of the independent variables. These can be used to directly compare the effects of each independent variable on our dependent variable, the political engagement scale. In addition, one-tailed t tests were performed to determine the statistical significance of the regression coefficients.

The results displayed in Table 2.4 indicate that after controlling for the other independent variables, the two race variables had negligible and statistically insignificant effects on political engagement. This means that any differences in political engagement between blacks and whites, or between other nonwhites and whites, were almost entirely a result of differences on the other independent variables such as age, education, and income. All of the other independent variables included in the regression analysis had statistically significant effects. However, the effects of gender and income were relatively small. After controlling for the other independent variables,

Table 2.4. Results of regression analysis of political engagement in 2004

Independent variable	Beta	t	Significance
Age	.225	8.22	<.001
Education	.218	7.16	<.001
Gender	−.100	−3.68	<.001
Black	.024	0.84	N.S.
Other race	−.009	−0.34	N.S.
Income	.072	2.38	<.01
Partisan intensity	.245	8.72	<.001
Ideological intensity	.277	9.10	<.001
Adjusted R^2 = .37			

Source: 2004 American National Election Study.

women and lower income individuals were only slightly less engaged in the political process than men or upper income individuals.

The strongest predictors of political engagement in 2004 were ideology and partisanship, followed closely by age and education. After controlling for the other independent variables, older and better educated Americans were considerably more engaged in the political process than younger and less educated Americans. In addition, after controlling for all of the other independent variables including age and education, strong liberals and conservatives were much more engaged in the political process than ideological moderates, and strong Democrats and Republicans were much more engaged in the political process than independents.

Explaining the Growth of Political Engagement in 2004: The Bush Effect

George W. Bush was the most polarizing presidential candidate in recent political history, and this was the main reason that the size of the engaged public increased dramatically in 2004. Bush was a much more polarizing figure than he had been four years earlier. Americans either loved him or hated him, and they went to the polls in record numbers to express those feelings. Voters' feelings about Bush were strongly related to their basic partisan and ideological orientations. Thus, the increasing polarization of the American electorate contributed to making Bush a divisive figure. However, the way the electorate perceived Bush changed dramatically between 2000 and 2004.

In the immediate aftermath of the terrorist attacks of September 11, 2001, Americans rallied behind President Bush as they had seldom rallied behind any modern president. After the attacks on New York and Washington, Bush received approval ratings of between 80 and 90 percent, with solid majorities of Democrats and independents as well as Republicans expressing support. By the fall of 2004, however, much of that support had dissipated. Although the large majority of Republicans continued to express strong support for the president, Bush's approval rating among Democrats was even lower that it had been before the September 11th attacks.

Evaluations of George Bush in 2004 were more divided along party lines than evaluations of any president since the ANES began asking the presidential approval question in 1972.[8] However, the highly polarized evaluations of Bush in 2004 represented a continuation of a trend that goes back at least thirty years. The difference between the percentage of Democratic identifiers and leaners and Republican identifiers and leaners approving of the president's job performance was 36 points for Richard Nixon in 1972, 42 points for Jimmy Carter in 1980, 52 points for Ronald Reagan in 1988, 55 points for George H. W. Bush in 1992 and Bill Clinton in 1996, and 71 points for George W. Bush in 2004. In an era of increasing partisan polarization, Bush set a new standard. In the 2004 ANES survey, 90 percent of Republicans approved of Bush's performance, and 81 percent of Democrats disapproved. Fully 66 percent of Republicans strongly approved of Bush's performance, and 64 percent of Democrats strongly disapproved.

Bush was evaluated very differently in 2004 as an incumbent president than he had been in 2000 as a presidential candidate. This can be seen by comparing the ratings of Bush on the ANES feeling thermometer scale during these two years. The feeling thermometer is a scale on which 0 degrees represents the lowest possible rating of an individual or group and 100 degrees represents the highest. Although the average rating of Bush on this scale was almost identical in both years—55 degrees in 2004 and 56 degrees in 2000—the two distributions differed dramatically. Bush was not an especially divisive figure during the 2000 campaign. The large majority of respondents in the ANES preelection survey rated him somewhere between cool (30 degrees) and lukewarm (70 degrees). Only a small minority expressed intensely positive or negative feelings. The standard deviation of the Bush feeling thermometer scale in 2000 was 24.6, slightly below the average for all presidential candidates since 1968 when the ANES introduced this item. In 2004, however, Bush was a divider. A majority of respondents rated him either below 20 degrees or above 90 degrees. The standard deviation of the Bush feeling thermometer scale in 2004 was 33.2, by far the largest of any presidential candidate since 1968.

A large part of the explanation for the increasingly polarized evaluations of George Bush was the increasingly divergent opinions held by liberals and conservatives and by Democrats and Republicans. Democrats rated him an average of 11 degrees lower in 2004 than in 2000, and Republicans rated him an average of 9 degrees higher. As a result, the difference between Democrats' and Republicans' ratings increased from 28 degrees in 2000 to 48 degrees in 2004. There was much less change in relative ratings of the Democratic candidates. Democrats rated John Kerry an average of 4 degrees lower than Al Gore, and Republicans rated Kerry an average of 9 degrees lower than Gore. As a result, the difference between Democrats' and Republicans' ratings only increased from 30 degrees in 2000 to 35 degrees in 2004.

A very similar pattern is seen when we compare the ratings of liberals and conservatives. Liberals rated Bush an average of 10 degrees lower in 2004 than in 2000, and conservatives rated him an average of 9 degrees higher. As a result, the difference between liberals' and conservatives' ratings increased from 26 degrees in 2000 to 46 degrees in 2004. Again, the relative ratings of the Democratic candidates changed much less. Liberals rated Kerry an average of 1 degree higher than Gore, and conservatives rated Kerry an average of 5 degrees lower than Gore. As a result, the difference between liberals' and conservatives' ratings increased from 24 degrees in 2000 to 30 degrees in 2004.

Further evidence of increasing partisan and ideological polarization in voters' evaluations of George Bush can be seen in Table 2.5, which displays the results of regression analyses of Bush feeling thermometer ratings in 2000 and 2004. The independent variables in the regression analyses were party identification and ideological identification along with several demographic control variables: age, gender, race, education, family income, marital status, and frequency of church attendance.

Table 2.5. Regression analyses of Bush feeling thermometer scores
in 2000 and 2004

Independent variable	2000	2004
Liberal-conservative identification	2.84 (.762)	3.72 (.727)
Party identification	5.44 (.525)	9.55 (.505)
Adjusted R^2	.375	.537

Source: 2000 and 2004 American National Election Studies.
Note: Entries are unstandardized regression coefficients with accompanying standard errors. Coefficients for demographic control variables are not shown.

The results in Table 2.5 show that the effects of both party identification and ideological identification on Bush evaluations increased dramatically between 2000 and 2004. The estimated unstandardized regression coefficient for ideological identification increased by more than 30 percent, and the estimated unstandardized regression coefficient for party identification increased by more than 75 percent. In addition, the overall explanatory power of the regression analysis increased dramatically. In 2000, the regression analysis explained only 37.5 percent of the variance in Bush evaluations; in 2004, it explained 53.7 percent of that variance.

In 2004, opinions about Bush were much more strongly influenced by voters' basic partisan and ideological orientations than they had been in 2000. According to these results, in 2000, a very conservative strong Republican would have rated Bush about 50 degrees higher than a very liberal strong Democrat—a substantial difference. In 2004, however, the Republican would have rated Bush about 80 degrees higher than the Democrat.

The intense polarization of voter opinion about President Bush was directly responsible for the extraordinarily high level of public engagement in the 2004 presidential election. The relationship between candidate and party polarization and participation has long been recognized by students of elections.9 The larger the difference that voters perceive between the candidates and parties, the greater their stake in the election outcome, and the more engaged in an election they are likely to be. In 2004, about 75 percent of Americans said that there were important differences between the parties, and about 85 percent said that they cared a good deal about who won the presidential election. Both of these figures were all-time records, breaking the previous records set during the 2000 campaign. By way of contrast, during the 1950s and 1960s, only about 50 percent of ANES respondents said that they perceived important differences between the parties, and only about 65 percent said that they cared a good deal about who won the presidential election.

Americans were more engaged in the 2004 presidential election than they had been in any presidential contest in the past fifty years. However, the high level of public engagement in the 2004 election represented a continuation of a trend that began during the 1980s and 1990s. As the Democratic and Republican parties have become more polarized and party identification in the electorate has become more consistent with ideological

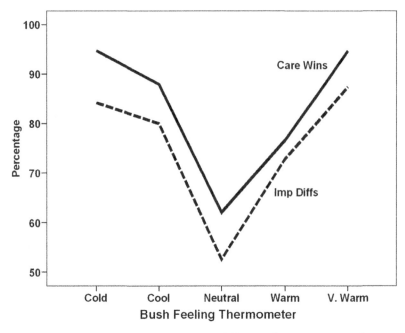

Figure 2.3. Percentages perceiving important differences between parties and caring who wins the presidential election in 2004 by rating of President Bush on the feeling thermometer (FT) scale. (*Source:* 2004 American National Election Study.)

identification and issue positions, supporters of the two parties have come to perceive a greater stake in the outcomes of elections.[10] For Democrats and Republicans alike, the difference between winning and losing an election is much greater than in the past because the differences between the parties' policies are much greater than in the past.

The extraordinary level of public engagement in the 2004 presidential election reflected the intense polarization of public opinion about George W. Bush. Figure 2.3 displays the relationship between two measures of engagement—perception of important party differences and concern about the winner of the election—and ratings of Bush on the feeling thermometer scale. The pattern is consistent with the polarization hypothesis: the more Americans liked or disliked Bush, the more engaged they were in the 2004 election. The most engaged members of the public were those who rated Bush below 30 degrees (cold) or above 80 degrees (very warm) on the feeling thermometer. These two groups made up more than half of the public. The least engaged members of the public were those who had a neutral evaluation of Bush (50 degrees). However, this group made up less than 10 percent of the public. It is clear that Americans in 2004 were deeply divided over Bush and his policies. Republicans overwhelmingly supported the president and his policies, Democrats overwhelmingly opposed the president and his policies, and both groups were energized by their belief in the importance of the choice facing the country.[11] The result was a substantial increase in the size of the engaged public.

Is Moderate Activism Possible?
A Look Back at the Perot Phenomenon

The evidence examined above indicates that political engagement among Americans increased dramatically in 2004 but that this increase was concentrated among those with strong partisan and ideological convictions. The level of political interest and activity was much lower among independents and moderates. One question that can be raised about these findings is to what extent the relatively low level of political engagement among independents and moderates in 2004 reflected the fact that there was no viable centrist candidate in the race. In order to examine the potential for moderate activism in the United States, we can look back at the last presidential election in which there was a viable moderate alternative to the two major party candidates—the 1992 election in which independent H. Ross Perot, running on a centrist platform emphasizing political reform and deficit reduction, garnered 19 percent of the national popular vote, which was the strongest showing for an independent or third-party candidate since 1912.[12]

An analysis of data from the 1992 ANES indicates that Perot's candidacy did, in fact, produce an increase in political engagement among independents and moderates. Perot supporters were just as likely to engage in campaign activities beyond voting as supporters of the two major party candidates, George H. W. Bush and Bill Clinton: 16 percent of Perot voters engaged in at least two activities beyond voting compared with 15 percent of Bush voters and 17 percent of Clinton voters. However, the Perot activists had a very different profile from the Bush and Clinton activists in terms of their partisan and ideological orientations. Only 15 percent of Perot activists were strong party identifiers compared with 54 percent of Bush activists and 48 percent of Clinton activists, and only 20 percent of Perot activists were strong liberals or conservatives compared with 46 percent of Bush activists and 55 percent of Clinton activists.

The Perot phenomenon provides evidence of both the potential for moderate activism in American politics and its limitations. Perot's candidacy helped to produce a dramatic surge in voter turnout in 1992. Moreover, the evidence from the 1992 ANES indicates that Perot voters were just as likely to engage in campaign activities beyond voting as supporters of the two major party candidates and that Perot activists, like Perot voters, were disproportionately moderates and independents. These findings suggest that under the right circumstances, a moderate independent or third-party candidate can increase the level of political engagement of moderate and independent voters. But by 1996, Perot's appeal had faded considerably. His second presidential bid attracted only 8 percent of the national popular vote, and turnout declined drastically. By the 2000 presidential election, most of those who had been active in Perot's presidential campaigns had either dropped out of politics or shifted their support to one of the two major parties, usually the Republicans.[13] And although there was considerable speculation about the possibility of an independent or third-party candidate running as a moderate alternative to the Democrats and Republicans in 2008, the decision by New York City mayor and billionaire Michael Bloomberg not to run meant that there would be no high-profile third-party or independent candidate in the race.

Ironically, the increased polarization of the two major parties since 1992 probably makes it more difficult for a moderate third-party or independent candidate to have the kind of effect that Ross Perot had. In general, the larger the policy differences between the parties, the more reluctant voters are to "waste" their vote on a third-party or independent candidate—the risk of helping to elect one's least preferred alternative simply becomes too great. So with the Democrats and Republicans now presenting the electorate with sharply opposing policy alternatives, and with the large majority of voters clearly aligned with one side or the other, there appears to be relatively little support among the public for a third-party or independent presidential candidate.[14]

Chapter Summary

Although scholars and pundits often depict ordinary Americans as having little interest in politics and public affairs and rarely engaging in political activities beyond voting, the reality described in this chapter is much more complex. We have seen that the American public is in fact quite diverse when it comes to political interest, knowledge, and participation. Many Americans have little or no interest in politics, know little about public affairs, and rarely bother to vote, but many others care deeply about politics, follow news about public affairs closely, and not only vote regularly but try to influence their friends' and neighbors' votes by talking to them during campaigns, displaying yard signs and bumper stickers, and contributing money to the parties and candidates. Moreover, the evidence presented in this chapter indicates that as the leaders and the Democratic and Republican parties have become increasingly polarized along ideological lines, interest in politics and participation in political activities have been increasing among the public.

In 2004, with the public deeply divided over the presidency of George W. Bush and the war in Iraq, voter turnout increased dramatically, as did participation in other election-related activities. In 2008, Bush was no longer on the ballot, but Barack Obama and John McCain presented Americans with sharply contrasting positions on almost every major domestic and foreign policy issue. Polling data and turnout in the presidential primaries and general election indicate that public interest in the 2008 presidential campaign was even higher than in 2004.

Some Americans may be turned off by the sharp ideological divisions between the parties, but more Americans appear to be excited and energized by the choice between a consistently liberal Democratic Party and a consistently conservative Republican Party. As a result, the size of the engaged public has been increasing. In the next chapter we examine the extent of partisan-ideological polarization within the public itself. We will see that the political attitudes of the engaged public resemble those of political elites.

3

Partisan-Ideological Polarization

THE IDEOLOGICAL SOPHISTICATION of the American public has been a subject of great interest to students of public opinion and voting behavior since the publication of Converse's study "The Nature of Belief Systems in Mass Publics." On the basis of his analysis of data from the 1956 and 1960 ANES, Converse concluded that the sort of ideological thinking common among political elites was confined to a small minority of the American public. The vast majority of ordinary voters showed little evidence of using an ideological framework to evaluate political parties or presidential candidates and very limited understanding of basic ideological concepts such as liberalism and conservatism. Perhaps most tellingly, the opinions expressed by citizens on current policy issues were almost completely unrelated. According to Converse, the absence of consistency, or constraint, in the opinions of ordinary voters proved that they were responding to these issues idiosyncratically, rather than on the basis of an underlying liberal or conservative ideology. In fact, on some issues Converse concluded that a majority of respondents did not even have meaningful opinions.[1]

Converse's findings concerning the absence of constraint and the prevalence of "nonattitudes" in public opinion on policy issues sparked considerable debate among students of public opinion in the United States. Christopher Achen argued that Converse's results reflected the poor quality of the questions used to measure policy attitudes in the early ANES surveys more than a lack of political sophistication on the part of ordinary Americans.[2] In addition, several studies of public opinion during the 1970s found that the level of ideological constraint was considerably greater than that observed by Converse.[3] However, other scholars concluded that much of this increase was due to changes in the questions used to measure issue positions in the ANES.[4]   *methodology, not major the chase*

Polarization as Constraint

The current debate over ideological polarization in the twenty-first-century American public is directly related to the earlier debate over constraint and ideological sophistication in the mid-twentieth-century American public. This is because constraint and polarization are closely related. In fact, one requires the other. For elites as well as for the mass public, ideological polarization is defined by consistency across issues; that is, the larger the proportion of leaders or citizens taking consistently liberal or conservative positions on issues, the higher the level of polarization. Ideological polarization in Congress is defined by consistency in voting across issues; ideological polarization in the public is defined by consistency in responses across survey items. This chapter addresses the question of how constrained and therefore how polarized the opinions of twenty-first-century American citizens are, particularly the opinions of those Americans who care about politics and participate regularly in the electoral process, that is, the engaged public.

Whatever the effects of changes in the ANES instrument, American politics and the American electorate have changed dramatically since the 1950s in ways that might lead one to expect an increase in the prevalence of ideological thinking in the public, as Converse himself has acknowledged.[5] One important change has been a substantial increase in the educational attainment of the electorate. In his original study, Converse found that education was a strong predictor of ideological sophistication: college-educated voters displayed much higher levels of ideological sophistication than grade school– or high school–educated voters. Between 1956 and 2004, the proportion of ANES respondents with only a grade school education fell from 37 percent to 3 percent while the proportion with at least some college education rose from 19 percent to 61 percent. On the basis of this trend alone,

one would expect a much larger proportion of today's voters to be capable of understanding and using ideological concepts.

Another development that might be expected to raise the level of ideological awareness among the public has been the growing intensity of ideological conflict among political elites in the United States. For several decades, Democratic officeholders, candidates, and activists have been moving to the left, while Republican officeholders, candidates, and activists have been moving to the right. Conservative Democrats and liberal Republicans, who were common in American politics during the 1950s and 1960s, are now extremely rare. At the elite level, ideological differences between the parties are probably greater now than at any time in the past half century.[6]

There is widespread agreement among scholars concerning the growing importance of ideological divisions at the elite level in American politics. There is much less agreement, however, about the significance of these divisions at the mass level. Some studies have found evidence that growing elite polarization has led to an increase in ideological awareness and polarization among the public.[7] Other scholars, however, most notably Morris Fiorina and his collaborators, have argued that when it comes to the political beliefs of the mass public, very little has changed since the 1950s. In his popular and influential book *Culture War? The Myth of a Polarized America,* Fiorina claims that Converse's portrait of the American electorate "still holds up pretty well." According to Fiorina, the ideological disputes that engage political elites and activists have little resonance among the American mass public: like their mid-twentieth-century counterparts, ordinary twenty-first-century Americans "are not very well-informed about politics, do not hold many of their views very strongly, and are not ideological."[8]

One major problem with such sweeping generalizations about the political sophistication of ordinary Americans is that ordinary Americans are far from homogeneous when it comes to political interest, knowledge, and activity.[9] Some have little or no interest in politics while others care deeply about political issues. Some know very little about government and politics while others know a great deal. And some don't bother to vote while others, as we have seen, not only vote but take part in other political activities. Any study of ideological sophistication in the public needs to take this diversity into account. As electoral competition in the United States has become increasingly structured by ideology, those citizens who lack a coherent ideological outlook may be increasingly alienated from the two major parties and from the electoral process itself. Thus, Fiorina's description of Americans as uninterested and nonideological may apply very well to the politically disengaged; however, it may not apply as well to politically engaged citizens, and it is the politically engaged whose opinions are of greatest concern to candidates and elected officials.

This chapter presents evidence that the American public has become more consistent and polarized in its policy preferences over the past several decades and that this increase in consistency and polarization has been concentrated among the most politically engaged citizens. Moreover, these engaged citizens are not a small, fringe group—they constitute a substantial proportion of the public and an even larger proportion of the actual electorate. This chapter also presents evidence that the increase in ideological consistency and polarization among the American public has been accompanied by a growing gap between the policy preferences of Democratic and Republican partisans. On a wide range of issues, rank-and-file Democrats and Republicans, like their elite counterparts, are much more divided today than in the past, and the sharpest divisions are found among the engaged partisans who comprise the electoral bases of the two parties.

These two processes—ideological polarization and party sorting—are in fact closely related. As the policy positions of Democratic and Republican leaders have become increasingly consistent and distinct, politically active citizens have responded by bringing their party identification into line with their policy preferences or by bringing their policy preferences into line with their party identification. The result has been growing consistency both across issues and between issue positions and party identification, a phenomenon that I call *partisan-ideological polarization*.

The Growth of Polarization in the American Public

A major problem in comparing the consistency of citizens' issue positions over time is that it is difficult to find issue questions that have been asked repeatedly over an extended period. One reason for this is that the major issues dividing the parties have changed with time. In addition, the

Table 3.1. Polarization on seven-item policy scale by political engagement,
1984–2004

	1984	1988	1992	1996	2000	2004	Change
Nonvoters	2.52	2.52	2.44	2.60	2.68	2.67	+6%
Voters	2.89	3.13	3.15	3.39	3.31	3.60	+25%
Active citizens	3.15	3.50	3.48	3.70	3.59	3.89	+23%
Campaigners	3.74	3.50	3.75	4.10	3.71	4.27	+14%

Source: American National Election Study Cumulative File.
Note: Entries are standard deviations of scores on a seven-item policy scale. Items included in
the scale are liberal-conservative identification, defense spending, abortion, aid to blacks, jobs
and living standards, health insurance, and spending versus services. Scores on the scale
range from −7 (consistently liberal) to +7 (consistently conservative). *Active citizens* are engaged in at least one activity beyond voting; *campaigners* are engaged in at least two activities
beyond voting.

format, wording, or both of many of the issue questions in the ANES surveys have changed. For example, the now familiar 7-point issue scales were
first introduced during the 1970s and 1980s. However, seven questions dealing with policy issues were included in every ANES presidential election
survey between 1984 and 2004. These questions asked about liberal versus
conservative identification, abortion policy, governmental aid to blacks, defense spending, government versus personal responsibility for jobs and living standards, government versus private responsibility for health insurance, and the trade-off between government services and spending. In order
to create a liberal-conservative policy scale, I coded responses to each of these
issue questions according to whether a respondent was on the liberal side,
the conservative side, or neither side (which included those in the middle
and those with no opinion) and combined them into a 15-point liberal-conservative policy scale with scores ranging from −7 for respondents who consistently took the liberal side on all seven issues to +7 for respondents who
consistently took the conservative side on all seven issues.

Figure 3.1. (Right) Polarization of voters on seven-item liberal-conservative policy
scale in 1984 and 2004. (*Source:* American National Election Studies.)

1984

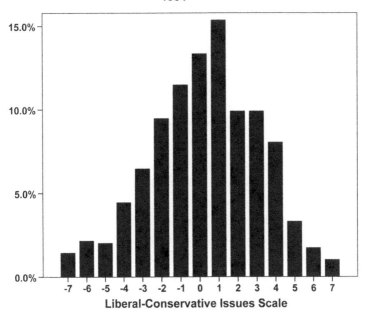

Liberal-Conservative Issues Scale

2004

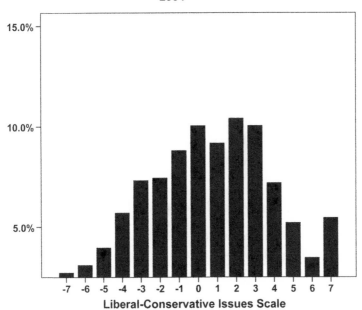

Liberal-Conservative Issues Scale

The standard deviation of the scores on the liberal-conservative policy scale can be used to measure the extent of ideological consistency and polarization within a group: the larger the standard deviation, the greater the dispersion of scores around the mean and therefore the greater the extent of consistency and polarization. Table 3.1 displays the standard deviation of scores on the liberal-conservative policy scale in 1984, 1988, 1992, 1996, 2000, and 2004 among four groups with varying levels of political engagement: nonvoters, voters, active citizens, and campaigners. *Active citizens* engaged in at least one activity beyond voting, and *campaigners* engaged in at least two activities beyond voting. The data show that in all six years, campaigners were the most polarized group, followed by active citizens, voters, and nonvoters. In addition, between 1984 and 2004, all four groups showed some increase in polarization. This increase among nonvoters was very slight, and the increases among voters and active citizens were much larger. According to these results, voters and active citizens were considerably more polarized in 2004 than they were in 1984.

To provide a sense of the significance of the increase in polarization between 1984 and 2004, Figure 3.1 shows the distribution of scores on the liberal-conservative policy scale among voters in each year. The two distributions look quite different. In 1984, 41 percent of voters were located within one unit of the center of the scale, and only 10 percent were located near the extremes on the left (−7 through −5) and right (5 through 7). In 2004, only 28 percent of voters were located within one unit of the center, and 23 percent were located near the left and right extremes. These results indicate that the 2004 electorate was much more consistent and polarized than the 1984 electorate. Although no direct comparison is possible, it seems reasonable to assume that the contrast would be even starker if we could compare the 2004 electorate with the 1956 electorate studied by Converse.

Political Engagement and Ideological Polarization in 2004

While the 2004 electorate was considerably more polarized than the 1984 electorate, ideological divisions were much greater among some types of voters than others. In order to measure ideological consistency and polarization among the American public in 2004, I created a scale based on re-

Table 3.2. Political engagement and ideological consistency in 2004

| | Ideological consistency (%) | | | |
	Low	Moderate	High	Total
Campaign interest				
Moderate to low	40	33	27	100
High	24	27	49	100
Political knowledge				
Low (0–4)	44	38	18	100
Moderate (5–7)	30	29	41	100
High (8–10)	15	19	66	100
Participation				
Low (0–1)	39	35	26	100
Moderate (2)	30	30	40	100
High (3+)	17	18	65	100

Source: 2004 American National Election Study.

sponses to sixteen issues included in the ANES. The issues ranged from government responsibility for jobs and living standards to gay marriage, health insurance, abortion, defense spending, and gun control; the scale has a reliability coefficient (Cronbach α) of .80. Scores on the original scale ranged from −16 for respondents who gave liberal responses to all sixteen issues to +16 for respondents who gave conservative responses to all sixteen issues. I then recoded the original 33-point scale into an 11-point scale for clarity in presentation.

Table 3.2 displays the relationship between ideological consistency and three measures of political engagement: interest, knowledge, and partici- pation.[10] The results show that it was the least interested, informed, and po- litically active Americans who were clustered around the center of the lib- eral-conservative spectrum. The more interested, informed, and politically active Americans were, the more likely they were to take consistently liberal or consistently conservative positions.

The implication of the findings in Table 3.2 is that the most politically en-

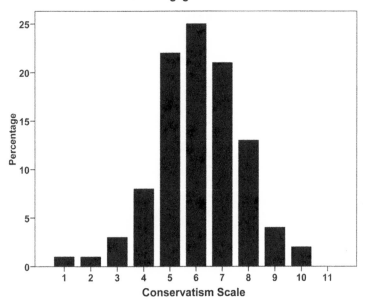

Least Engaged Third

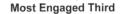

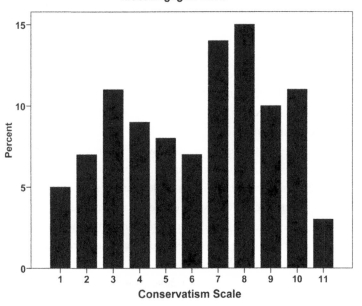

Most Engaged Third

more bimodal w/ information

gaged citizens are also the most polarized in their political views. In order to directly test this hypothesis, I combined the political interest, knowledge, and participation scales to create an overall index of political engagement. I then divided the respondents in the 2004 ANES sample into three groups of approximately equal size: the least politically engaged, a middle group, and the most politically engaged. The politically engaged group included 37 percent of all respondents in the survey and close to half of the voters.

Figure 3.2 displays the ideological orientations of the least politically engaged and most politically engaged groups. As hypothesized, the high-engagement group was much more polarized in its policy preferences than the low-engagement group. Although the means of the two distributions are almost identical (6.1 and 6.2), the standard deviation of the high-engagement group (2.8) is almost twice as large as that of the low-engagement group (1.5). Very few individuals in the low-engagement group had consistent policy preferences: 13 percent were consistent liberals (1–4), and 19 percent were consistent conservatives (8–11). In contrast, a large proportion of individuals in the high-engagement group had fairly consistent policy preferences: 32 percent were consistent liberals, and 39 percent were consistent conservatives.

These results indicate that the engaged public is in fact quite polarized in its political attitudes. This fact has important political implications because candidates and elected officials are likely to be more concerned about the views of the politically engaged than about those of the politically disengaged. It is the politically engaged who pay attention to the positions that candidates and officeholders take and who consistently turn out to vote in primaries and general elections.

The Growth of Partisan-Ideological Polarization

The political significance of ideological polarization, however, does not depend on just the overall distribution of political attitudes among the public

Figure 3.2. (Left) Comparison of ideological orientations of least politically engaged group with most politically engaged group, 2004. Based on eleven-item liberal-conservative scale. (*Source:* 2004 American National Election Study.)

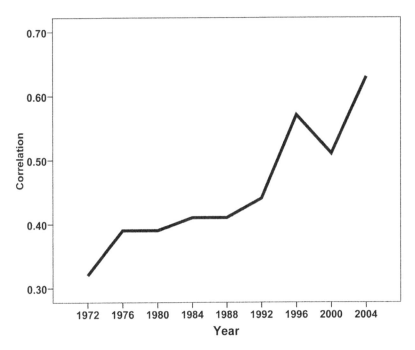

Figure 3.3. Correlation of party identification with liberal-conservative identification, 1972–2004. *Note:* Correlation coefficient is Pearson *r* based on 7-point party identification scale and 7-point liberal-conservative identification scale. (*Source:* American National Election Studies.)

or even among the politically engaged segment of the public. It also depends on the extent to which the ideological divisions within the public coincide with partisan divisions, or on partisan-ideological polarization. The greater the degree of partisan-ideological polarization in a society, the greater the likelihood that ideological differences will be expressed in the political arena and therefore the greater the intensity of political conflict in that society.

Evidence from the ANES indicates that partisan-ideological polarization has increased considerably over the past several decades. Figure 3.3 displays the trend in the correlation between liberal-conservative identification and party identification between 1972, when the ideology question was first included in the ANES, and 2004. This graph shows that the strength of the relationship between party identification and ideological identification has in-

Table 3.3. Trends in partisan polarization on issues, 1972–2004

Issue	1972–1980	1984–1992	1996–2004
Aid to blacks	.20	.27	.35
Abortion	−.03	.08	.18
Jobs/living standards	.28	.34	.40
Health insurance	.25	.31	.39
Liberal-conservative identification	.42	.49	.62
Presidential approval	.42	.56	.61
Average	.26	.34	.43

Source: American National Election Studies.
Note: Entries shown are average correlations (Kendall τ) between issues and party identi-
fication (strong, weak, and independent Democrats versus strong, weak, and independent
Republicans).

creased substantially since 1972 and especially since 1992. In 1972, the correlation between ideology and party identification was .32; in 1992, it was
.44; and in 2004, it was .63. In statistical terms, this means that the strength
of this relationship almost quadrupled: the proportion of variance that these
two questions had in common increased from just over 10 percent in 1972
to almost 40 percent in 2004. As a result, the difference between the mean
score of Democratic identifiers and that of Republican identifiers on the 7-
point liberal-conservative identification scale increased from 0.9 units in
1972 to 1.3 units in 1992 and 1.8 units in 2004. Given the limited range of
this scale, this is a substantial increase in polarization; the gap between
Democratic and Republican identifiers doubled between 1972 and 2004.

The increase in partisan polarization was not limited to the liberal-conservative identification question. Differences between Democratic and Republican identifiers have increased substantially over the past three decades
on a wide range of issues. Table 3.3 displays the correlations between party
identification and positions on six items—aid to blacks, abortion, jobs and
living standards, health insurance, liberal-conservative identification, and
presidential approval—during 1972–1980, 1984–1992, and 1996–2004:
the larger the correlation coefficient, the greater the degree of partisan po-

larization on an item. On every one of these items, partisan polarization increased substantially.

Evaluations of presidential performance have become increasingly polarized along party lines since the 1970s, with evaluations of George W. Bush in 2004 especially so. According to data from the 2004 ANES, 90 percent of Republican identifiers approved of Bush's performance, and 66 percent approved strongly; in contrast, 81 percent of Democratic identifiers disapproved of Bush's performance, and 64 percent disapproved strongly. Evaluations of Bush were more divided along party lines than those of any president since the ANES began asking the presidential approval question in 1972. However, these highly polarized evaluations of Bush were not unique; they represented a continuation of a trend that goes back several decades: the difference between the percentage of Democratic identifiers and Republican identifiers approving of the president's performance was 36 points for Richard Nixon in 1972, 42 points for Jimmy Carter in 1980, 52 points for Ronald Reagan in 1988, 55 points for George H. W. Bush in 1992 and Bill Clinton in 1996, and 71 points for George W. Bush in 2004.

These results indicate that the growing partisan divide in presidential evaluations cannot be explained by changes in the leadership styles or policies of the presidents themselves. Bill Clinton ran and governed as a moderate Democrat, yet evaluations of his performance were much more sharply divided along party lines than evaluations of the performance of earlier presidents. And in many ways, Richard Nixon was at least as divisive a figure as George W. Bush, yet the partisan divide in evaluations of Nixon was only half as large as that in evaluations of Bush. The dramatic increase in partisan polarization between these two presidents reflects the fact that the American public has changed and that Democratic and Republican identifiers now hold much more consistent and polarized views across a wide range of policy issues than their counterparts during the 1960s and 1970s.

Further evidence for this conclusion can be found in public evaluations of Barack Obama during the first few weeks of his presidency. Despite his oft-repeated promise to change the tone in Washington from the bitter partisanship of the Bush years and his well-publicized efforts to reach out to congressional Republicans, one month into his presidency, opinions of Obama's performance were already sharply divided along party lines. In a

Fox News Poll conducted February 17–18, 2009, Obama received a 90 percent approval rating from Democrats but only a 29 percent approval rating from Republicans. Although Obama's overall approval rating of 60 percent was substantially higher than President Bush's approval ratings during his final years in office, the 61-point gap between Democrats and Republicans was almost as large as the partisan gap in ratings of Bush, who was widely viewed as one of the most divisive presidents in the modern era.

Political Engagement and Partisan-Ideological Polarization in 2004

The evidence from the 2004 ANES shows that partisan polarization was not confined to a small group of leaders and activists. The ideological preferences of rank-and-file Democratic and Republican identifiers (including leaning independents) actually differed rather sharply. Democratic identifiers tended to be fairly liberal while Republican identifiers tended to be fairly conservative. This is clear when we compare the distribution of Democratic and Republican identifiers on the 11-point liberal-conservative issue scale. The mean scores on the scale were 5.0 for Democrats compared with 7.5 for Republicans. This difference is highly statistically significant ($p <$ .001), as well as substantively significant. Fifty-six percent of Democrats were on the liberal side of the scale (1–5) compared with only 12 percent of Republicans; 73 percent of Republicans were on the conservative side of the scale (7–11) compared with only 21 percent of Democrats.

Partisan-ideological polarization was considerably greater among the engaged public than among the entire public. The mean scores on the 11-point liberal-conservative scale were 3.8 for politically engaged Democrats compared with 8.3 for politically engaged Republicans—almost twice as large as the difference between all Democratic and Republican identifiers. This difference is both substantively and statistically significant ($p <$ .001). Eighty-two percent of politically engaged Democrats were on the liberal side of the scale (1–5) compared with only 7 percent of politically engaged Republicans; 91 percent of politically engaged Republicans were on the conservative side of the scale (7–11) compared with only 12 percent of politically engaged Democrats.

There were large differences between the positions of politically engaged

Table 3.4. Policy liberalism among politically engaged partisans in 2004

Issue	Democrats (%)	Republicans (%)
Abortion	67	25
Death penalty	52	10
Diplomacy vs. force	74	15
Environment vs. jobs	74	27
Gay marriage	69	18
Jobs/living standards	52	9
Health insurance	66	16
Spending/services	65	18

Source: 2004 American National Election Study.

Democrats and Republicans on a wide range of specific issues in 2004. Some of these issue differences are displayed in Table 3.4. On every one of the eight issues included in the table, politically engaged Democrats were much more liberal than politically engaged Republicans. This was true on social, economic, and foreign policy issues. The smallest differences, 42 percentage points, were on the issues of abortion and the death penalty. The largest difference, 59 percentage points, was on the use of military force versus diplomacy in the conduct of foreign policy. Across these eight issues, an average of 65 percent of politically engaged Democrats took the liberal position compared with an average of 17 percent of politically engaged Republicans.

Politically engaged partisans have always been more polarized along ideological lines than ordinary party identifiers. However, like ordinary party identifiers, politically engaged partisans have become increasingly polarized over time. In order to measure political engagement between 1972 and 2004, I created an additive scale based on one question asking about interest in the campaign, one question asking how much respondents cared about the outcome of the presidential election, and an index of campaign activities. I coded those who scored at the upper end of this scale as politically engaged. The proportion of respondents classified as politically engaged ranged from 12 percent in 1956 to 26 percent in 2004.

Between 1972 and 2004, the correlation (Pearson r) between party identification and ideological identification among the most politically engaged citizens increased from .47 to .77. As a result, the difference between the average score of politically engaged Democrats and that of politically engaged Republicans on the 7-point liberal-conservative scale increased from 1.4 units in 1972 to 2.7 units in 2008. The level of polarization among politically engaged partisans in 2004 was the highest in the history of the ANES despite the fact that the proportion of citizens classified as politically engaged was also the highest in the history of the ANES.

Evidence from the Cooperative Congressional Election Study

The remainder of this chapter uses another data set, the 2006 Cooperative Congressional Election Study (CCES), to present additional evidence about ideological constraint and polarization in the contemporary American electorate. The CCES involved an Internet-based survey of voting-age Americans conducted by Polimetrix, Inc., on behalf of a consortium of scholars at thirty-seven colleges and universities. Polimetrix uses a sample-matching methodology to produce a sample that is representative of the overall U.S. electorate.[11] Registered voters were deliberately oversampled in order to ensure adequate coverage of different types of House and Senate contests: the CCES surveyed more than thirty-six thousand eligible voters, including more than twenty-four thousand who reported voting in the 2006 midterm election.

In order to assess the validity of the evidence from the CCES survey, I compared the characteristics of voters in the CCES sample with those of voters in the 2006 National Exit Poll (NEP). On most characteristics, including race, gender, and income, the CCES sample was very similar to the NEP sample. Most importantly, the party division of the vote for the House of Representatives in the CCES sample was identical to that in the NEP sample and matched the actual party division of the vote in the election. On a few characteristics, however, the two samples differed. Compared with the NEP sample, the CCES sample included a smaller proportion of respondents older than sixty, a larger proportion of respondents with only a high school education, and a smaller proportion of college graduates. The CCES sample

P did not include questions that would allow one to
measure ideological constraint or polarization. However, none of the differences between the CCES sample and the NEP sample would lead one to
expect CCES respondents to be more ideologically sophisticated or more
polarized in their issue positions than NEP respondents. If anything, the
smaller proportion of college graduates and the larger proportion of independents in the CCES sample would lead one to expect a lower level of ideological sophistication and a lower degree of ideological polarization among
CCES respondents than among NEP respondents. It seems reasonable,
therefore, to treat the CCES voter sample as representative of the actual
midterm electorate in terms of ideological sophistication and polarization.

Ideological Constraint and Polarization in 2006

When asked about their political views, more Americans generally describe themselves as moderate or middle-of-the-road than as either liberal or
conservative, and this was true of respondents in both the CCES and the
2006 NEP. With regard to ideological identification, the results of the two
surveys were very similar. In both surveys, the moderate category was the
most popular, and self-identified conservatives outnumbered self-identified
liberals. In the 2006 NEP, 45 percent of respondents described themselves
as moderate, 21 percent as liberal, and 34 percent as conservative. The results were slightly different in the CCES survey because the CCES gave respondents five categories to choose from instead of only three. Just as in the
NEP, however, far more CCES respondents placed themselves in the moderate category (38 percent) than in any other single category, and self-identified conservatives (38 percent) outnumbered self-identified liberals (24 percent).

On the basis of their ideological self-identification, CCES respondents,
like voters responding to the 2006 NEP, and like respondents in almost
every other recent national opinion poll, appear to be a predominantly moderate group. Almost two-fifths of voters in the CCES survey placed themselves exactly in the center of the 5-point liberal-conservative scale while less

than one-fifth placed themselves at either the left or right extremes. But liberal-conservative self-identification is only one measure of political ideology. The fact that the moderate label is very popular with American voters does not necessarily mean that the electorate is predominantly moderate, any more than the popularity of the independent label means that the electorate is predominantly independent. Political scientists have learned that many self-described independents, on closer inspection, turn out to have a clear partisan orientation.[12] Similarly, many self-described moderates may turn out to have a clear ideological orientation.

In order to measure the degree of ideological constraint and polarization in the 2006 electorate, I analyzed the answers provided by CCES respondents to twelve questions, eleven dealing with current national issues, as well as the ideological identification question. The eleven issues included in this analysis were abortion, partial birth abortion, stem cell research, social security privatization, the minimum wage, environmental protection versus job protection, affirmative action, capital gains taxes, immigration, and two questions about the war in Iraq, one about whether the war had been a mistake and the other about the withdrawal of U.S. troops.[13] These issues cover a variety of policy domains—cultural and economic, as well as foreign and domestic. One question asking about the Central American Free Trade Agreement (CAFTA) was dropped from the analysis because responses did not correlate very highly with responses to any of the other issues in the survey. Two other issues, gay marriage and global climate change, were dropped because the questions about these issues were asked only of a subsample of respondents who were not, in other respects, representative of the entire sample.

Table 3.5 displays the correlations (Pearson r) among responses to the twelve questions in the CCES for two groups of respondents: voters and nonvoters. All of the items are coded in a consistent direction, from the most liberal response to the most conservative response, so that a positive correlation indicates consistency. The results in the table show that there was an impressive degree of constraint in the opinions of voters. The average correlation among their responses to these twelve questions was .47. In contrast, the opinions of nonvoters demonstrated a much lower degree of constraint. The average correlation among their responses to the same twelve

Table 3.5. Product-moment correlations among twelve questions
in the Cooperative Congressional Election Study

	Abortion	Affirm. action	Cap. gains taxcut	Environ. vs. jobs	Libcon ID	Immigration	Iraq withdraw	Iraq mistake	Min. wage	Partial birth	SS private	Stem cell
A. Voters												
Abortion	1.000	.364	.431	.417	.575	.289	.473	.548	.382	.602	.478	.634
Affirm. action	.364	1.000	.448	.405	.503	.412	.451	.494	.428	.370	.474	.407
Cap. gains taxcut	.431	.448	1.000	.455	.537	.300	.559	.590	.483	.430	.611	.501
Environment vs. jobs	.417	.405	.455	1.000	.487	.313	.455	.505	.430	.401	.487	.468
Libcon ID	.575	.503	.537	.487	1.000	.395	.563	.621	.478	.510	.545	.586
Immigration	.289	.412	.300	.313	.395	1.000	.318	.362	.287	.287	.298	.317
Iraq withdraw	.473	.451	.559	.455	.563	.318	1.000	.715	.535	.437	.578	.557
Iraq mistake	.548	.494	.590	.505	.621	.362	.715	1.000	.520	.505	.653	.617
Minimum wage	.382	.428	.483	.430	.478	.287	.535	.520	1.000	.353	.504	.494
Partial birth	.602	.370	.430	.401	.510	.287	.437	.505	.353	1.000	.479	.524
SS private	.478	.474	.611	.487	.545	.298	.578	.653	.504	.479	1.000	.541
Stem cell	.634	.407	.501	.468	.586	.317	.557	.617	.494	.524	.541	1.000

B. Nonvoters

	Abortion	Affirm. action	Cap. gains taxcut	Environ. vs. jobs	Libcon ID	Immigration	Iraq withdraw	Iraq mistake	Min. wage	Partial birth	SS private	Stem cell
Abortion	1.000	.101	.141	.135	.403	.105	.187	.265	.115	.429	.197	.478
Affirm. action	.101	1.000	.188	.126	.259	.268	.189	.227	.217	.130	.134	.146
Cap. gains taxcut	.141	.188	1.000	.178	.255	.061	.237	.239	.232	.147	.251	.149
Environment vs. jobs	.135	.126	.178	1.000	.254	.169	.146	.214	.164	.146	.131	.214
Libcon ID	.403	.259	.255	.254	1.000	.214	.278	.358	.222	.300	.205	.373
Immigration	.105	.268	.061	.169	.214	1.000	.112	.183	.104	.117	.082	.140
Iraq withdraw	.187	.189	.237	.146	.278	.112	1.000	.445	.305	.144	.197	.240
Iraq mistake	.265	.227	.239	.214	.358	.183	.445	1.000	.179	.237	.297	.266
Minimum wage	.115	.217	.232	.164	.222	.104	.305	.179	1.000	.058	.201	.205
Partial birth	.429	.130	.147	.146	.300	.117	.144	.237	.058	1.000	.164	.304
SS private	.197	.134	.251	.131	.205	.082	.197	.297	.201	.164	1.000	.148
Stem cell	.478	.146	.149	.214	.373	.140	.240	.266	.205	.304	.148	1.000

Source: 2006 Cooperative Congressional Election Study.
Note: Libcon ID indicates liberal-conservative identification; SS, social security.

questions was only .20. Clearly, the opinions of voters on national issues were much more constrained than the opinions of nonvoters.

The correlations among the issue positions of voters in the 2006 CCES were not only much stronger than those of nonvoters, they were also much stronger than the correlations among the issue positions of either the public or the sample of congressional candidates analyzed by Converse.[14] When the opinions of the CCES voter sample on these twelve items were subjected to a principal component factor analysis, the first dimension extracted by the factor analysis had an Eigen value of 6.3 and explained 52 percent of the common variance, and no other factor had an Eigen value of greater than 1.0. The average correlation between the twelve items and the first factor was a robust .72. Moreover, according to an internal consistency analysis, a simple additive scale based on these twelve items had a Cronbach α value of .90, well beyond what is generally considered necessary for a satisfactory scale.

These analyses indicate that there is an ideological structure to the opinions of voters which is very similar to that of voting in Congress: the responses of voters to these twelve questions largely reflected their positions on a single underlying liberal-conservative dimension just as the votes of members of Congress largely reflect their positions on a single underlying liberal-conservative dimension.[15]

There is a very close relationship between constraint and polarization in public opinion: the larger the average correlation among the opinions in a group, the larger the proportion of consistent liberals and consistent conservatives in that group. Thus, on the basis of the correlations in Table 3.5, I would expect the opinions of voters to be much more polarized than the opinions of nonvoters; this difference is clearly evident in Figure 3.4, which compares the distributions of voters and nonvoters on the twelve-item liberal-conservative scale.

The difference between the two distributions is striking. The opinions of voters follow a bimodal distribution, whereas the opinions of nonvoters follow a unimodal distribution. Only 17 percent of voters fall in the center (between 40 percent conservative and 60 percent conservative) of the distri-

Figure 3.4. (Right) Distributions of voters and nonvoters on liberal-conservative issue scale in 2006. (*Source:* 2006 Cooperative Congressional Election Study.)

Voters

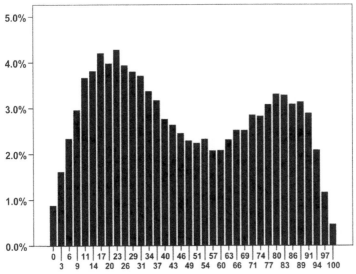

Liberal-Conservative Scale

bImodal
for voters

Non-Voters

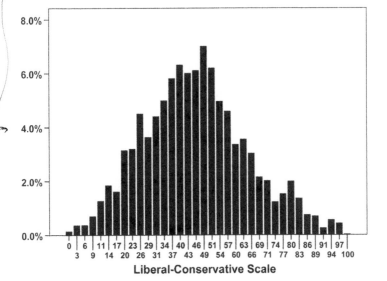

Liberal-Conservative Scale

Unimodal for -nvoters

bution while 39 percent of voters fall at either the left (less than 20 percent conservative) or the right (80 percent conservative to 100 percent conservative) ends of the scale. In contrast, 41 percent of nonvoters fall in the center of the distribution, and only 12 percent fall at the left or right ends of the scale. On the basis of these results, Fiorina's characterization of the American public as nonideological appears to apply much better to nonvoters than to voters. The large majority of voters in 2006 held fairly consistent opinions on a wide range of national issues. Moreover, these opinions were strongly related to their candidate preferences: voters at the left end of the scale voted almost unanimously for Democratic House and Senate candidates, and voters at the right end of the scale voted almost unanimously for Republican House and Senate candidates. In contrast, the minority of voters in the middle of the scale, those whose opinions were the least consistent, divided their support fairly evenly between the two major parties.

The result of the voting patterns was a very high level of ideological differentiation between Democratic and Republican voters in 2006. There was very little overlap between the two groups of voters on the liberal-conservative scale: 89 percent of Democratic House voters were located to the left of center, and 84 percent of Republican House voters were located to the right of center. Democratic House voters had an average score of 28 percent conservative on the scale, and Republican House voters had an average score of 70 percent conservative. The Senate pattern was even stronger: 91 percent of Democratic Senate voters were located to the left of center, with 88 percent of Republican Senate voters located to the right of center. Democratic Senate voters had an average score of 27 percent conservative on the scale, and Republican Senate voters had an average score of 72 percent conservative. Moreover, the ideologies of Democratic and Republican voters were almost identical in every region of the country. The average score of Democratic House voters was 29 percent conservative in the South, 28 percent conservative in the Northeast, 29 percent conservative in the Midwest, and 25 percent conservative in the West. The average score of Republican House voters was 69 percent conservative in the South, 70 percent conservative in the Northeast, 70 percent conservative in the Midwest, and 72 percent conservative in the West.

There were sharp differences between Democratic and Republican voters on every one of the issues included in the liberal-conservative scale. The largest differences between Democratic and Republican voters in 2006 were over the war in Iraq. Eighty-six percent of Democratic House voters considered the war a mistake compared with only 17 percent of Republican House voters, and 83 percent of Democratic House voters favored a proposal to immediately begin withdrawing U.S. troops from Iraq compared with only 25 percent of Republican House voters. There were also differences of more than 50 percentage points on such issues as stem cell research, social security private accounts, and capital gains tax cuts. The smallest difference between Democratic and Republican voters was found on the issue of immigration. Even here, however, there was a difference of 38 percentage points between Democratic and Republican House voters in support for a proposal to allow illegal immigrants to obtain U.S. citizenship. The dramatic differences between the views of Democratic and Republican voters on a wide range of cultural, economic, and national security issues indicate that partisan-ideological polarization in Congress does not exist in a vacuum. Democrats and Republicans in Congress appear to be accurately reflecting the views of their supporters in the electorate.

Partisan-Ideological Polarization in 2006

Recent elections have seen a resurgence of partisanship in the American electorate. The proportion of pure independents in the electorate has been declining since the 1970s while the level of partisan voting has been increasing.[16] The evidence from the CCES indicates that these trends continued in 2006. According to the CCES data, 91 percent of the voters in the 2006 House and Senate elections identified with or leaned toward one of the two major parties. Ninety percent of Democratic identifiers and leaners and 85 percent of Republican identifiers and leaners voted for their own party's House candidate; 94 percent of Democratic identifiers and leaners and 87 percent of Republican identifiers and leaners voted for their own party's Senate candidate.

A large part of the explanation for the high level of partisan voting in 2006 and other recent elections is the high level of consistency between party identification and ideology in the American electorate. Among voters in the CCES survey, 94 percent of Democratic identifiers and leaners were found on the left side of the liberal-conservative scale, and 88 percent of Republican identifiers and leaners were found on the right side of the scale. Ninety-two percent of liberal Democrats and 90 percent of conservative Republicans voted for their own party's House candidate. In contrast, only 56 percent of conservative Democrats and 48 percent of liberal Republicans voted for their own party's House candidate. Similarly, 96 percent of liberal Democrats and 94 percent of conservative Republicans voted for their own party's Senate candidate, and only 63 percent of conservative Democrats and 47 percent of liberal Republicans voted for their own party's Senate candidate.

Figure 3.5 displays the average score of voters on the liberal-conservative scale in relation to the 7-point party identification scale. These results go a long way toward explaining why independent leaders behave much more like partisans than like pure independents. Independent Democrats ("Lean

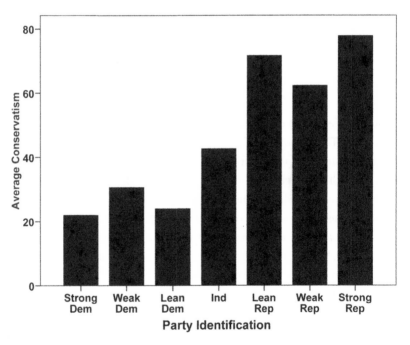

Figure 3.5. Average score of voters on liberal-conservative scale in relation to the party identification scale. (*Source:* 2006 Cooperative Congressional Election Study.)

Dem" on the figure) were considerably more liberal than weak Democrats and almost as liberal as strong Democrats. Similarly, independent Republicans ("Lean Rep") were considerably more conservative than weak Republicans, although not as conservative as strong Republicans. Ideologically, these independent leaners were much more similar to their co-partisans than to each other. These findings suggest that the high level of party loyalty of independent leaners in 2006 and other recent elections is based on their ideological orientations, not just on a short-term preference for one party or the other. Thus, the findings support the conclusion of Keith et al. that independent leaners should be considered partisans rather than independents.[17]

The role of ideology and social background characteristics in the development of partisan identity has been a subject of debate among political scientists.[18] In order to address the issue of the centrality of ideology to partisan identity in the American electorate, I conducted a discriminant analysis of party identification among voters in the CCES survey using ideology and a wide variety of social background characteristics, including age, race, gender, education, family income, religion, marital status, and church attendance, to predict Democratic versus Republican identification. On the basis of our earlier results indicating that independent leaners should be considered partisans rather than independents, independent leaners were combined with strong and weak identifiers into the two partisan groups. The results of the discriminant analysis are displayed in Table 3.6.

Overall, the variables included in the discriminant analysis correctly classified 91.7 percent of Democratic and Republican identifiers. However, an examination of the standardized canonical discriminant function coefficients in Table 3.6 shows that one variable had far greater predictive power than any other: ideology. In fact, the liberal-conservative scale alone correctly predicted the party identification of 91.3 percent of voters in the CCES survey. In contrast, all of the social background variables together correctly predicted the partisan identification of only 70.6 percent of voters. Social characteristics added almost no predictive power to ideology alone. On the basis of these results, ideology appears to be much more central to voters' partisan identities than social characteristics such as class, gender, and race.

Table 3.6. Results of discriminant analysis of 2006 party identification

Social background characteristic	Coefficient
Age	.025
Education	.096
Gender	−.024
Family income	.071
Marital status	.007
Race	
Black	−.159
Hispanic	−.013
Other	−.013
Religion	
Catholic	−.058
Jewish	−.022
Other	−.033
No religion	−.038
Church attendance	−.030
Ideology	.977
Canonical correlation = .831	
Percentage correctly classified = 91.7	

Source: 2006 Cooperative Congressional Election Study.
Note: Standardized canonical discriminant function coefficients are shown. Predicted groups are strong, weak, and independent Democrats versus strong, weak, and independent Republicans.

Chapter Summary

American politics has changed dramatically in the half century since Philip Converse conducted his path-breaking research on belief systems in mass publics. The educational level of the American electorate has risen steadily. Just as importantly, ideological conflict among political elites has greatly intensified. The findings presented in this chapter indicate that these changes have had profound consequences for electoral competition in the United States. To a considerable extent, electoral competition is now structured by ideology. Voters with relatively coherent ideological preferences choose between parties with relatively clear and distinct ideological positions. At least on the electoral side, the conditions for responsible party government have largely been met.

It is important to recognize, however, that the conclusions of this chapter regarding the role of ideology in structuring mass political behavior in the United States apply mainly to the politically engaged segment of the public. Data from the 2004 ANES and the 2006 CCES indicate that ideological constraint and polarization were much greater among voters than among nonvoters. Whether the lack of consistency evident in the opinions of nonvoters reflects fundamental cognitive limitations, lack of interest in the issues that dominate the contemporary political agenda, or genuine ambivalence about these issues remains unclear. As the role of ideological conflict in the electoral process increases, however, there is a risk that those citizens who for whatever reason lack a consistent ideological outlook will become increasingly alienated from the two major parties and from the electoral process itself. The American public appears to be increasingly divided into two groups: the politically engaged, who view politics in ideological terms, and the politically disengaged, who do not.

4

Polarization and Social Groups

FOLLOWING HIS VICTORY IN THE 1932 presidential election, Franklin Delano Roosevelt forged an electoral coalition that dominated American politics for the next thirty-six years. Between 1933 and 1969, the Democratic Party controlled the presidency for twenty-eight years and both chambers of Congress for thirty-two years. During these years Democrats also controlled a majority of the nation's governorships and state legislative chambers along with most other state and local elected offices.[1]

Democrats dominated American politics during these years because they enjoyed the support of a large majority of American voters, as the authors of *The American Voter* discovered when they undertook their pioneering national surveys during the 1950s and 1960s. In 1952, for example, even as Republican Dwight Eisenhower was winning a landslide victory in the presidential election, 56 percent of American voters identified with or leaned toward the Democratic Party compared with only 39 percent who identified with or leaned toward the Republican Party. While Republicans were able to hold on to some of their traditional state and local strongholds in the aftermath of the New Deal realignment, the GOP could win national elections during these years only when short-term forces in their favor were strong enough to overcome the Democrats' substantial lead in party identification within the American electorate.

Roosevelt's electoral coalition was based primarily on group loyalties, some of whose origins could be traced back to events that occurred long before the New Deal, and secondarily on the widespread association of the Democratic Party with prosperity and the Republican Party with economic hardship in the aftermath of the Great Depression. Ideology was a relatively minor component of party identification at the mass level during these years, as the authors of *The American Voter* documented. When Americans were asked in 1956 what they liked or disliked about the Democratic and Republican parties, only a small minority mentioned the parties' ideological stances. The large majority of positive and negative comments about the parties fell into two other categories: group benefits (approximately 40 percent) and the nature of the times (approximately 25 percent).[2]

The major groups comprising Roosevelt's New Deal coalition were white voters in the South and white ethnic (largely Catholic) and working-class voters in the North.[3] Black voters, who had been strong supporters of the Republican Party in the decades after the Civil War and Reconstruction, also began to shift their loyalties to the Democrats during the 1930s, but they did not become a major component of the Democratic electoral coalition until the mid-1960s when the passage of the 1965 Voting Rights Act finally made it possible for large numbers of blacks in the South to register and vote.[4]

What brought these disparate groups of voters together under the Democratic umbrella was a common perception that the Democrats served the interests of each group better than the Republicans. That was the gist of most of the answers to the questions about party likes and dislikes that fell into the "group benefits" category. More than two decades after the onset of the Great Depression and Roosevelt's ascension to the presidency, the authors of *The American Voter* found that most Americans still viewed the Democrats as the party of the working class and the average citizen, whereas they viewed the Republicans as the party of big business and the wealthy.[5]

Among white voters in the South and white ethnic voters in the North, the Depression and Roosevelt's New Deal reinforced longstanding ties to the Democratic Party. For most southern whites during the 1950s, the Republican Party was viewed not only as the party responsible for the Great Depression, which hit the South harder than any other region of the country, but also as the party that imposed Reconstruction on the South and granted voting rights to blacks after the Civil War.[6] And for most white ethnic voters in the North, the Democratic Party was viewed not only as the party that offered jobs and hope during the Depression, but as the party that welcomed immigrants from Ireland and from southern and eastern Europe during the nineteenth and early twentieth centuries.[7]

The continuing loyalty of these groups to the Democratic Party is clearly evident in the data from the 1952 ANES, which was the first one to include the standard party identification questions. Among all voters in 1952, Democratic identifiers and leaners outnumbered Republican identifiers and leaners by 56 percent to 39 percent; among southern whites, however, Democratic identifiers and leaners outnumbered Republican identifiers and leaners by 84 percent to 14 percent; among northern white Catholics, Democratic identifiers and leaners outnumbered Republican identifiers and leaners by 68 percent to 26 percent; and among northern white blue-collar voters, Democratic identifiers and leaners outnumbered Republican identifiers and leaners by 60 percent to 33 percent. The Republican Party did remain dominant during this period among middle-class white Protestants outside of the South. Among these voters, Republican identifiers and leaners outnumbered Democratic identifiers and leaners by 66 percent to 30 percent. But this group was simply too small to allow Republicans to win national elections or even to win elections in most states.

The Decline of the New Deal Coalition

The New Deal coalition kept the Democrats in power in Washington and in most of the states for the better part of four decades. But it was inherently unstable, made up of groups that not only varied in political outlook, but in some cases mistrusted and disliked each other. Cracks began to form in this coalition shortly after Roosevelt's death in 1945. In 1948 South Carolina governor J. Strom Thurmond led a walkout from the Democratic national convention over its adoption of a weak civil rights plank and ran for the presidency as the candidate of the States Rights, or Dixiecrat, Party. Thurmond carried several states in the Deep South, but Democratic president Harry S. Truman was reelected anyway. Four years later, however, Dwight Eisenhower broke the Democratic grip on the White House and became the first Republican since 1928 to carry any of the states of the old Confederacy by winning the electoral votes of Virginia, Tennessee, Florida, and Texas. Eisenhower carried all of these states again, along with Louisiana, in his successful bid for reelection in 1956.

The movement of southern white voters away from the Democratic Party accelerated during the 1960s and 1970s with the Democrats' embrace of civil rights and the Republicans' adoption under Richard Nixon of a "southern strategy" that combined opposition to busing and affirmative action with a get-tough approach to antiwar protesters and urban rioters.[8] As the evidence presented in the first graph of Figure 4.1 shows, even the election of a Democratic president from the Deep South, Jimmy Carter of Georgia, in 1976, could not stop the erosion of support for the Democratic Party among southern white voters.

The southern strategy was designed to win over the large bloc of voters in the South who had supported the independent candidacy of former Alabama governor George Wallace in 1968. But the Republican Party's conservatism on racial and cultural issues did not appeal just to southern whites. It also appealed to many white ethnic and working-class voters in the North who were becoming increasingly uncomfortable with the liberalism of the national Democratic Party on these issues and its growing dependence on the support of black voters. Many of these traditional Democrats voted for Richard Nixon over George McGovern in 1972, and many of them also voted for Ronald Reagan in 1980 and 1984.

Reagan's ascension to the presidency in 1981 accelerated the process of ideological realignment that had begun under Nixon. Reagan cemented the GOP's ties to socially conservative white evangelicals, a large voting bloc in the South, by attacking Supreme Court decisions legalizing abortion and banning school prayer. But he also appealed to many white voters in the North who applauded his efforts to strengthen the U.S. military and stand up to the Soviet Union and who were upset about welfare programs that they believed primarily benefited blacks who were unwilling to work.[9]

The graphs displayed in Figure 4.1 document the dramatic decline in support for the Democratic Party among the three groups that formed the core of Roosevelt's New Deal coalition: white voters in the South and white Catholics and working-class voters in the North. The largest decline in Democratic identification occurred among the group with the longest-standing

Regional Differences among White Voters

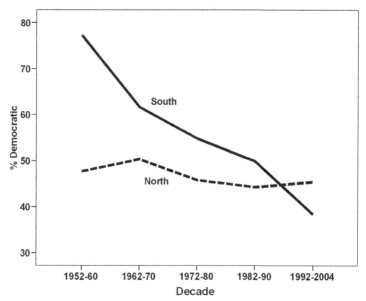

Class Differences among Northern White Voters

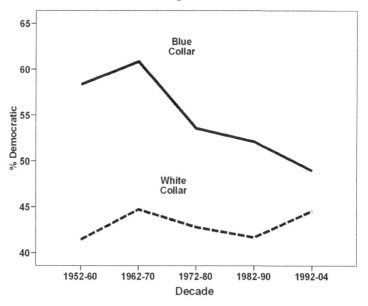

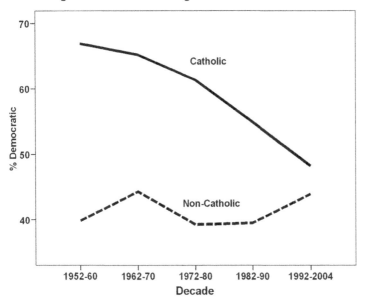

Figure 4.1. (Left and above) The decline of the New Deal coalition.
(*Source:* American National Election Studies.)

ties to the Democratic Party—white southerners. Between the 1950s and
the 1990s, Democratic identification among this group fell from close to
80 percent to less than 40 percent. During the same years, Democratic identification among white voters outside of the South declined only slightly. As
a result, by the 1990s Democratic identification among white voters in the
South was actually lower than Democratic identification among white voters outside of the South.

According to the data displayed in the second graph of Figure 4.1, the decline in Democratic identification among working-class whites in the North
began later than the decline among whites in the South. As late as the
1960s, more than 60 percent of white blue-collar voters in the North continued to identify with the Democratic Party. The data show that during the
1950s and 1960s, class differences in party identification were still quite evident among white voters in the North. During these years there was a difference of at least 15 percentage points in Democratic identification between

blue-collar voters and white-collar voters. Over the next three decades, however, this gap diminished dramatically as a result of a sharp decline in Democratic identification among white working-class voters. By the 1990s, Democratic identification had fallen below 50 percent among white working-class voters in the North. Meanwhile, Democratic identification among white middle-class voters remained fairly stable at around 45 percent, only a few percentage points lower than among white working-class voters. Although class differences in party identification did not disappear, they did become much smaller than in the years immediately following World War II.

The third major group that helped the Democrats dominate American politics from the 1930s through the 1960s was white ethnic voters in the North. The large majority of these voters were Roman Catholics whose parents or grandparents had arrived in the United States during the massive waves of immigration of the late nineteenth and early twentieth centuries and had settled in the rapidly growing cities of the Northeast and Midwest —cities whose local governments were generally controlled by the Democratic Party.

As was the case for white voters in the South, the Great Depression and the New Deal reinforced the loyalty of white ethnic voters in the North to the Democratic Party. These voters gave massive majorities to Franklin D. Roosevelt in each of his four elections, and in 1960 Catholic voters provided John F. Kennedy, the first Roman Catholic presidential candidate since Al Smith in 1928, with an overwhelming majority of their votes. According to the 1960 ANES, 82 percent of white Catholic voters supported Kennedy over his Republican opponent, Richard Nixon.

Between 1952 and 1960, as shown in the third graph of Figure 4.1, almost two-thirds of white Catholic voters in the North identified with the Democratic Party. By contrast, during those years only 40 percent of non-Catholic white voters in the North identified with the Democrats. These data underscore how crucial the Catholic vote was to the Democratic Party in the North during the postwar years. Over the next three decades, however, Democratic identification among northern white Catholics declined steadily, falling below 50 percent during the 1990s. By that time, white Catholics were only slightly more supportive of the Democratic Party than white non-Catholics, and another pillar of the New Deal coalition had crumbled.

Explaining the Demise of the
New Deal Coalition: Ideological Realignment

[handwritten margin note: shift of group to ideology]

The collapse of support for the Democratic Party among southern whites, northern white working-class voters, and northern white ethnic voters had a common cause: ideological realignment. This is clear from the three graphs displayed in Figure 4.2, which show the trends in Democratic identification among liberals, moderates, and conservatives between the 1970s and the first decade of the twenty-first century. The first graph shows the trends for southern white voters, the second for northern white working-class voters, and the third for northern white Catholic voters.

In all three groups, Democratic identification declined only slightly among moderates and remained stable or increased among liberals. In all three groups, the decline in Democratic identification between the 1970s and the first decade of the twenty-first century was concentrated almost entirely among conservatives. Among conservative southern whites, identification with the Democratic Party fell from 40 percent during the 1970s to less than 10 percent in 2002–2004; however, among moderate southern whites, Democratic identification only fell from 60 percent to 50 percent, and among liberal southern whites, Democratic identification actually rose from 70 percent to 80 percent. The results were very similar for white working-class and Catholic voters in the North. Among conservative white working-class voters, Democratic identification fell from close to 40 percent during the 1970s to less than 10 percent in 2002–2004; however, among moderate working-class voters, Democratic identification only fell from 55 percent to 45 percent, and among liberal working-class voters, it remained stable at close to 80 percent. Finally, among conservative white Catholics, Democratic identification fell from just under 40 percent during the 1970s to about 10 percent in 2002–2004. Among moderate white Catholics, Democratic identification only fell from a little over 60 percent to about 50 percent, and among liberal white Catholics, it rose from just over 80 percent to close to 90 percent.

By the end of the twentieth century, the process of ideological realignment was almost complete among the politically engaged segment of the electorate, and the old New Deal coalition had largely disintegrated. There

White Southerners

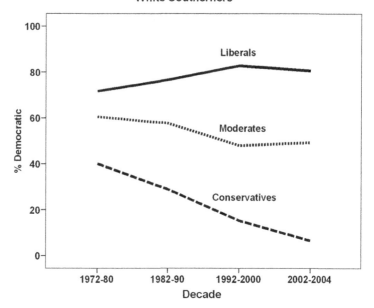

Northern White Blue Collar Workers

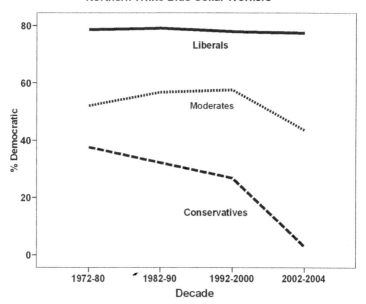

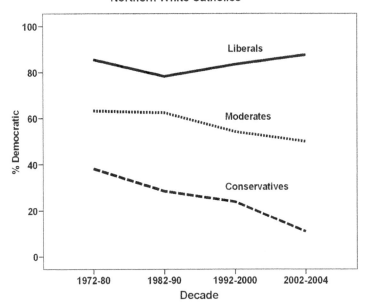

Figure 4.2. (Left and above) The ideological realignment of the New Deal coalition. (*Source:* American National Election Studies.)

were almost no conservative Democrats left, and the two parties were at near parity in party identification. In the elections of the first decade of the twenty-first century, a predominantly liberal Democratic Party supported by close to half of the electorate would oppose a predominantly conservative Republican Party supported by close to half of the electorate. Within this evenly divided electorate, however, new group divisions had emerged to replace the old divisions of region, class, and religion.

The Racial Divide

The most important divide within the contemporary electorate, because of its historical significance, its magnitude, and its influence on many other aspects of American politics, is the racial divide. The Great Depression and Franklin Roosevelt's New Deal brought African Americans into the Democratic electoral coalition for the first time since the Civil War. But as recently as 1960, the Republican Party continued to enjoy significant support among African American voters. In that year's presidential election, according to the ANES, Richard Nixon received 26 percent of the black vote against John F. Kennedy. However, no Republican presidential candidate since then has approached that share of the black vote. Despite the increasing social and economic diversity of the black electorate, in the first decade of the twenty-first century, African Americans remain the most solidly Democratic voting bloc in the nation.

The data displayed in Figure 4.3 show that identification with the Democratic Party among African American voters increased from about 70 percent during the 1950s to close to 90 percent from the 1960s through the 1990s. Meanwhile, Democratic identification among white voters fell from just over 50 percent during the 1950s and 1960s to just over 40 percent dur-

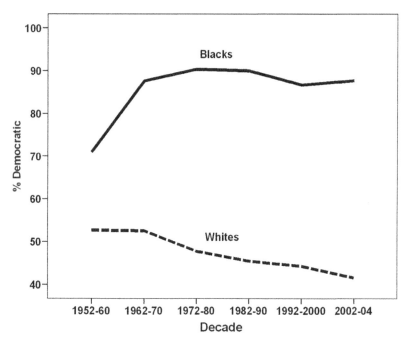

Figure 4.3. The growing racial divide in partisanship.
(*Source:* American National Election Studies.)

ing the 1990s. A 20-point racial divide in partisanship during the 1950s had grown to 50 points during the 1980s and 1990s.

The reason for the dramatic increase in the size of the racial divide in partisanship after 1960 was, of course, the emergence of a clear difference between the Democratic and Republican parties on civil rights and other racially charged issues such as busing, affirmative action, crime, and welfare.[10] The same issues that drove many conservative white voters into the arms of the Republican Party during the 1960s, 1970s, and 1980s caused the large majority of African American voters to view the GOP as unsympathetic to black people at best and racist at worst. As a result, no Republican presidential candidates, and very few Republican Senate and House candidates, have received much more than 10 percent of the black vote in any election since 1960.

The racial divide in partisanship is even deeper in the South, the region that continues to have by far the highest proportion of black voters, than in the rest of the country. In 2002–2004, according to ANES data, the Democratic Party was supported by 86 percent of black voters versus 44 percent of white voters in the North—a gap of 42 percentage points. During the same period, the Democratic Party was supported by 89 percent of black voters versus only 33 percent of white voters in the South—a gap of 56 percentage points. In some parts of the South, especially in the Deep South where blacks make up a third or more of the electorate, the racial divide in partisanship is so great that the Republican Party has come to be viewed as the white political party and the Democratic Party as the black political party.

As barriers to the social and economic advancement of African Americans have gradually come down over the past several decades, the black population of the United States has become increasingly diverse. Although Africans Americans are still an economically disadvantaged group, a large black middle class has developed in the nation's major metropolitan areas, and African Americans are increasingly found in professional and managerial occupations.[11] In addition, in recent years an influx of immigrants from the African continent and the Caribbean has added to the diversity of America's black population.[12]

Surprisingly, however, this growing diversity has not led to growing diversity in the partisan orientations of African American voters. Despite recent efforts by the Republican Party to reach out to the black community and the presence of several African Americans in key leadership positions in the Bush administration, black voters in the United States have remained steadfastly loyal to the Democratic Party. In 2004, according to NEP data, almost 90 percent of African Americans voted for Democrat John Kerry over President Bush. Moreover, the data displayed in Table 4.1 show that during the years 1992–2004, the Democratic Party remained dominant in every

Table 4.1. Democratic identification among African
American voters, 1992–2004

	Democratic (%)
Age	
18–29	87
30–39	84
40–49	85
50–64	89
65+	89
Gender	
Male	84
Female	89
Education	
High school	84
Some college	92
Graduated college	86
Family income	
Lower third	86
Middle third	88
Upper third	87
Ideology	
Liberal	96
Moderate	85
Conservative	73

Source: American National Election Study Cumulative File.

major subgroup within the African American community. Younger blacks were just as Democratic as older blacks; black college graduates were just as Democratic as blacks with only a high school education; and upper income blacks were just as Democratic as lower income blacks. Black men were slightly less Democratic than black women, and black conservatives were somewhat less Democratic than black moderates and liberals, but even these differences were fairly minor. It is striking that almost three-fourths of black conservatives, a group whose political outlook might have been expected to make them more sympathetic to the Republican Party's message, continued to identify with the Democratic Party during these years.

These findings suggest that the racial divide is different from every other social divide in the United States. For African Americans, in contrast to every other major social group in the country, partisanship remains rooted in group identity rather than in ideology. The large majority of African Americans continue to perceive the Republican Party as unsympathetic, if not hostile, to the needs and concerns of black people—a perception that was reinforced by the Bush administration's response to devastation caused by Hurricane Katrina in 2005, which some critics believe was inept and influenced by racial and class prejudice.[13] As long as that perception remains, it is likely that black voters will continue to overwhelmingly identify with the Democratic Party and vote for Democratic candidates, from the presidency down to the local level. The nomination and election of Barack Obama, the nation's first African American president, clearly has reinforced the loyalty of African American voters to the Democratic Party. According to the 2008 NEP, African Americans made up a record 13 percent of the national electorate and cast 95 percent of their votes for Obama. As long as Obama is in the White House, the prospect of Republican inroads among African American voters would appear to be remote.

The New Divides among White Voters: Gender, Marriage, and Religious Commitment

Since the 1970s, as traditional group loyalties forged during the New Deal and earlier faded in importance, several new divisions have developed among white voters. The most significant are the gender gap, the marriage

The Gender Gap

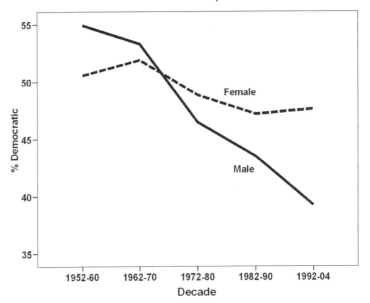

The Marriage Gap

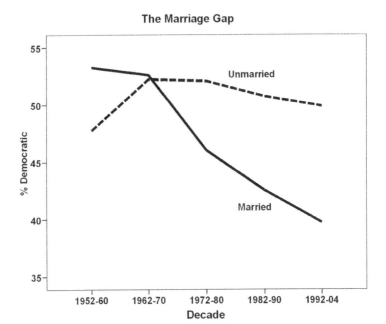

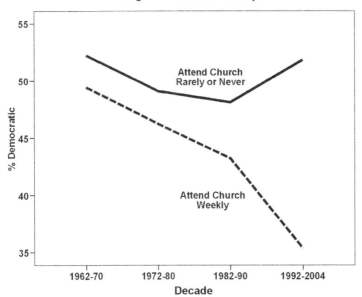

Figure 4.4. (Left and above) New group divisions among white voters: gender, marriage, and religious commitment. (*Source:* American National Election Studies.)

gap, and the religious commitment gap. The emergence of these divisions can be seen very clearly in the three graphs of Figure 4.4, which display the trends in Democratic identification over the past thirty to forty years among white male and female voters, white married and single voters, and white religious and nonreligious voters.

The gender gap has received perhaps the greatest attention from political scientists and journalists since its initial appearance in the 1970s. Over the past three decades, the fact that white women are more likely to identify with the Democratic Party and vote for Democratic candidates at all levels than white men has been frequently noted.[14] What the data displayed in the first graph of Figure 4.4 make clear, however, is that the gender gap was not a result of growing affection for the Democratic Party among white women; instead, it developed because support for the Democratic Party declined less drastically among white women than among white men. It was for this reason that a gender gap of between 5 and 10 percentage points in party identification was evident by the beginning of the twenty-first century.

A similar phenomenon is evident when we examine the development of the marriage gap among white voters.[15] The data displayed in the second graph of Figure 4.4 show that before the 1970s, there was little or no difference in party identification between single and married white voters. But since the 1970s, single white voters have consistently supported the Democratic Party to a greater extent than married white voters. As in the case of the gender gap, however, the marriage gap emerged not because of an increase in support for Democrats among single voters but because of the fact that support for Democrats declined less dramatically among single voters than among married voters. As a result, a marriage gap of more than 10 percentage points in party identification had developed by the beginning of the twenty-first century.

Perhaps the most politically significant division among white voters today, however, is the religious commitment gap. And once again, as the third graph of Figure 4.4 shows, this gap is of relatively recent origin. Before the 1980s there was very little difference in party identification between religious and nonreligious white voters; religious voters were only slightly less likely to identify with the Democratic Party than nonreligious voters. Starting in the 1980s, however, something happened to increase the salience of religious commitment in the political arena, and by the turn of the twenty-first century, the religious commitment gap among white voters was even larger than the gender gap or the marriage gap.[16] According to the data displayed in this graph, in the most recent period, more than half of nonreligious white voters identified with the Democratic Party compared with barely a third of religious white voters.

This religious commitment gap developed during the 1980s and 1990s because the Democratic and Republican parties became increasingly associated with opposing positions on issues that tended to divide voters according to their religious beliefs and practices, such as abortion, school prayer, public subsidies for religious schools, and, later, gay rights.[17] This process began during the 1980s with Ronald Reagan speaking out against Supreme Court decisions banning school prayer and legalizing abortion and culminated during the 2004 presidential election with George W. Bush's advocacy of a constitutional amendment to ban same-sex marriage. By that time, however, the increasingly close relationship between the Republican Party and the religious right had begun to produce a backlash among more moderately religious and secular voters that is evident in the graph. Between the 1980s and the 1990s, Democratic identification fell by 8 percentage points among religious whites but rose by 5 percentage points among nonreligious whites.

In the 2004 presidential contest, religious commitment was a much stronger predictor of the vote among whites than social class. This can be seen in Figure 4.5, which displays the joint effects of family income and church attendance on the presidential vote among whites. The results indicate that among both frequent and infrequent churchgoers, support for President Bush was only slightly higher among upper income voters than among lower income voters. Within every income category, however, support for Bush was substantially greater among frequent churchgoers than in-

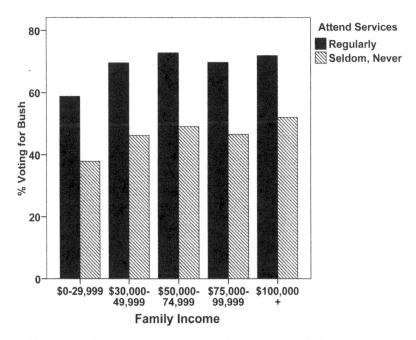

Figure 4.5. Religious commitment versus class: percentage of whites voting for Bush in 2004 by family income and church attendance. (*Source:* 2004 National Exit Poll.)

frequent churchgoers. The average difference in support for Bush within each income category was close to 20 percentage points. Support for Bush was actually greater among frequent churchgoers with family incomes less than $30,000 than among infrequent churchgoers with family incomes of $100,000 or more: a large majority of low-income churchgoers voted for Bush, while a majority of wealthy non-churchgoers voted for Kerry.

Among white voters today, the religious divide appears to be considerably wider than the class divide. The evidence from the 2008 presidential election provides additional support for this conclusion. Despite the fact that many white evangelical voters had deep misgivings about John McCain's candidacy, and few members of this group supported him in the Republican primaries, McCain received the overwhelming majority of votes from white evangelicals in the November election. According to the 2008 NEP, 74 percent of white evangelicals cast their ballots for McCain, down only slightly from the 78 percent who voted for Bush in 2004.

All of these divides within the white electorate—the gender gap, the marriage gap, and the religious commitment gap—made their first appearance during the 1970s or 1980s, and all reached their largest size within the past decade. This is because these divides are by-products of growing partisan-ideological polarization. Over the past three decades, the Democratic Party has moved to the left and the Republican Party has moved to the right on racial, cultural, and economic issues. As a result, groups with more conservative views on these issues such as men, married voters, and religious voters have been increasingly attracted to the Republican Party, whereas groups with more liberal views on these issues such as women, single voters, and nonreligious voters have found the Republican approach much less appealing.

The crucial role ideology plays in producing these new divides within the white electorate is evident in Table 4.2, which displays the relationship between party identification and gender, martial status, and church attendance among white voters while controlling for ideology. The results indicate that all three gaps disappear after controlling for ideology. Liberal, moderate, and conservative men are just as likely to identify with the Democratic Party as liberal, moderate, and conservative women; liberal, moderate, and conservative married voters are just as likely to identify with the Democratic Party

Table 4.2. Explaining the gaps: Democratic identification by ideology
among white voters, 1992–2004

	Liberal (%)	Moderate (%)	Conservative (%)
Gender			
Male	78	52	21
Female	78	50	24
Marital status			
Married	76	50	21
Single	80	52	26
Church attendance			
Weekly or more	78	52	24
Seldom or never	80	48	22

Source: American National Election Study Cumulative File.

as liberal, moderate, and conservative single voters; and liberal, moderate, and conservative churchgoers are just as likely to identify with the Democratic Party as liberal, moderate, and conservative non-churchgoers.

Because the gender, marriage, and religious commitment gaps are themselves by-products of more fundamental ideological divisions within the electorate, the size of these gaps should vary with the level of political engagement of citizens. The largest gaps should be found among the most politically engaged members of the public because, as we have seen, the link between ideology and party identification is strongest among the most politically engaged citizens. And that is exactly what Table 4.3 shows: the gender, marriage, and religious commitment gaps are all considerably larger among the most politically engaged citizens than among the least politically engaged citizens.

The effect of political engagement is particularly striking when it comes to religious commitment. In the low engagement group, the difference in party identification between frequent and infrequent churchgoers is relatively small: there is a 21-point Democratic advantage among infrequent church-

Table 4.3. Political engagement and group differences in party identification among whites, 1992–2004 (% Democratic − % Republican)

	Low engagement	High engagement
Female	+17	+4
Male	+11	−16
Difference	+6	+20
Single	+20	+13
Married	+10	−21
Difference	+10	+34
Infrequent churchgoers	+21	+15
Frequent churchgoers	+5	−31
Difference	+16	+46

Source: American National Election Study Cumulative File.

goers compared with a 5-point Democratic advantage among frequent church-goers. In the high engagement group, however, the difference in party iden-tification between frequent and infrequent churchgoers is much larger: there is a 15-point Democratic advantage among infrequent churchgoers compared with a 31-point Republican advantage among frequent churchgoers. Although Democrats slightly outnumbered Republicans among the least politically en-gaged religious whites, Republicans outnumbered Democrats by a two-to-one margin among the most politically engaged religious whites. This find-ing calls into question the claim that the Republican Party has made gains among religious white voters by duping the most politically naive members of this group into voting against their own self-interest.[18] In fact, Republican gains among religious white voters have been concentrated among the most politically sophisticated members of this group.

Chapter Summary

The electoral coalitions supporting the Democratic and Republican par-ties have undergone a dramatic transformation over the past half century. By the beginning of the twenty-first century, the three major pillars of the coalition forged by Franklin D. Roosevelt during the Depression years—white southerners and white working-class and ethnic voters in the North—had largely collapsed. As a result of defections by self-identified conservatives, Democratic identification within each of these groups fell steadily from the 1960s through the 1990s until by the end of the century there were almost no conservative Democrats left.

The disintegration of the New Deal coalition was accompanied by the emergence of new divisions within the electorate—divisions based on race, gender, marital status, and religious commitment. During the 1960s and 1970s, as the national Democratic Party embraced the cause of civil rights and the Republican Party began aggressively courting racially and culturally conservative whites in the South and elsewhere, African Americans went from being a solidly Democratic voting bloc to being an overwhelmingly Democratic voting bloc. Meanwhile, within the white electorate, groups with conservative views on racial and cultural issues such as men, married voters, and frequent churchgoers shifted their loyalties to the Republicans while groups with more liberal views on these issues such as women, single voters, and infrequent churchgoers continued to support the Democrats.

The end result of all of these changes has been the emergence of a new American party system—one in which party loyalties are based primarily on voters' ideological beliefs rather than on their membership in social groups. This transformation of the party system has had profound consequences for almost every aspect of the electoral process in the United States, as we will see in the next chapter.

5

Polarization and Elections

GROWING PARTISAN-IDEOLOGICAL polarization has had important consequences for almost every aspect of the electoral process in the United States.
It has affected voter turnout and the composition of the electorate, party loyalty and defection, the prevalence of ticket splitting, competition in presidential and congressional elections, the campaign strategies of politicians,
and competition in primary elections. In this chapter I examine these
changes and explain why, as a result of increasing partisan-ideological polarization, an electoral process characterized by candidate-centered campaigns aimed primarily at persuading swing voters has been transformed
into one characterized by party-centered campaigns aimed primarily at mobilizing core party supporters.

Partisan-Ideological Polarization and Voter Turnout

Why does anyone vote? Millions of Americans troop to the polls every two
years to cast ballots in thousands of contests for local, state, and federal offices, but political scientists have long been puzzled about why so many people bother to make the effort. From an economic standpoint, the costs of
voting appear to vastly outweigh the benefits. The time and effort required
for registering, learning about the candidates and issues, traveling to the
polls on Election Day, and waiting in line to cast a ballot would seem to
greatly exceed the benefits of helping one's preferred candidate to win since

the probability that a single vote will alter the outcome of any election is vanishingly small.[1]

The solution to this puzzle, according to scholars, is that citizens are not deterred from voting by the long odds against casting the deciding vote in an election because they receive intangible psychological rewards from the act of voting itself. Back in the 1950s and 1960s, students of voting behavior believed that the principal psychological reward citizens derived from the act of voting was satisfying a sense of civic duty. Americans, according to this argument, were taught in their homes and high school civics classes that voting was a fundamental responsibility of citizenship, and they felt guilty if they did not fulfill this responsibility.[2] Therefore, they could be counted on to go to the polls in large numbers even if they did not think their vote would be decisive and even if they did not think that it would make much difference which candidate or party won an election. And, indeed, studies of voting behavior during the 1950s and 1960s found that most Americans did consider voting a fundamental responsibility of citizenship and that a sense of civic duty was a strong predictor of turnout.[3]

Voter turnout was relatively high in the elections of the 1950s and 1960s even though, in many of these elections, the differences between the presidential candidates and the two major parties on domestic and international issues were fairly small or nonexistent. In fact, some scholars during that era believed that "the end of ideology" had arrived in American politics and that the major problems confronting the nation could be dealt with on a bipartisan basis through the application of scientific knowledge and technical expertise.[4]

But that was then, and this is now. The "end of ideology" theory came crashing to earth during the 1960s and 1970s as first the issue of civil rights and then the war in Vietnam produced deep divisions within the political establishment and the electorate. These divisions cut across party lines, and they instigated a process of ideological realignment at both the elite and mass levels.[5] Conservative Democrats found themselves increasingly uncomfortable in a party committed to civil rights for African Americans and an expanded welfare state, and liberal Republicans found themselves increasingly uncomfortable in a party committed to courting conservative white voters in the South and elsewhere by opposing civil rights legislation and any expansion of social welfare programs.[6]

As a result of this ideological realignment, today the two major parties in the United States present voters with a stark choice between opposing political philosophies. But how have voters responded to this realignment? One important change has involved the motivations for voting itself. Americans no longer vote primarily to satisfy a sense of civic duty; the primary motivation for voting today appears to be partisanship: Americans vote because they enjoy helping their party's candidates to defeat the opposing party's candidates.

Figure 5.1 displays the trend in voter turnout in presidential elections since the 1950s among strong partisans, weak and independent partisans, and pure independents according to ANES data. Although survey respondents tend to exaggerate the rate at which they vote and engage in other political activities, the data provide us with a lengthy time series that can be used to compare turnout rates of different groups in the population. And in

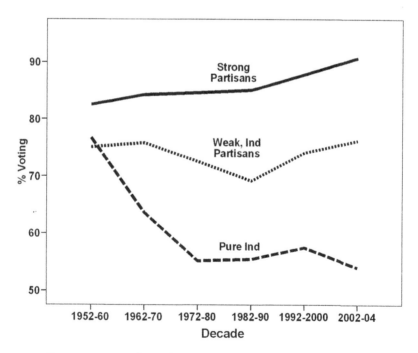

Figure 5.1. Partisanship and turnout in presidential elections by decade.
(*Source:* American National Election Studies.)

this case, the comparison shows a dramatic change in relative turnout rates of these groups since the 1950s.

During the 1950s, the relationship between partisanship and turnout was weak: strong partisans voted at only a slightly higher rate than weak and independent partisans or pure independents. Since then, however, the gap in turnout between these groups has increased considerably. The reported turnout rate among pure independents has fallen from close to 80 percent during the 1950s to just over 50 percent in recent years. Meanwhile, the reported turnout rate among strong partisans has increased from about 80 percent during the 1950s to almost 90 percent in the 2004 presidential election.

The dramatic decline in reported turnout among pure independents suggests that civic duty is no longer as potent a motivation for voting as it was in the past. Without the incentive of partisanship, these individuals perceive little stake in the outcome of elections and feel little reason to go to the polls. In contrast, because the differences between the parties and candidates are much greater than in the past, strong partisans now perceive a greater stake in the outcomes of elections than in the past and have more reason than ever to go to the polls.

Evidence supporting this explanation of the increasing relationship between partisanship and turnout is displayed in Figure 5.2, which shows the trend in the average absolute difference between ratings of the Democratic and Republican presidential candidates on the ANES feeling thermometer scale among three types of voters: strong partisans, weak and independent partisans, and pure independents. Since scores on the feeling thermometer scale range from 0 to 100, the largest possible difference between one's ratings of the candidates is 100 degrees. The larger the difference between one's ratings of the candidates, the more strongly one prefers one candidate to the other and, presumably, the larger the stake one should perceive in the outcome of an election.

Figure 5.2 shows that since the 1960s the trends in the intensity with which different groups of partisans prefer the candidate of one party to that of the other have diverged dramatically. During the 1960s, the average difference between strong partisans and pure independents on this scale was relatively small. On average, strong partisans rated their preferred candi-

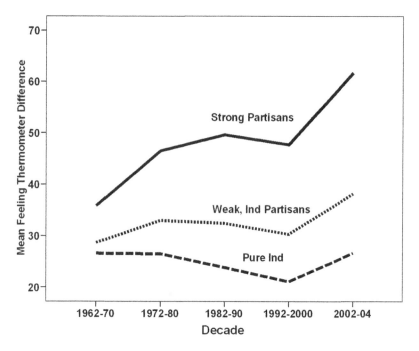

Figure 5.2. Partisanship and ratings of presidential candidates on the feeling thermometer scale by decade. (*Source:* American National Election Studies.)

date about 35 degrees higher than the opposing candidate while pure independents rated their preferred candidate about 25 degrees higher than the opposing candidate. By 2004, however, strong partisans rated their preferred candidate more than 60 degrees higher than the opposing candidate while pure independents still rated their preferred candidate about 25 degrees higher than the opposing candidate.

Between the 1960s and 2004, the average difference between ratings of one's preferred candidate and the opposing candidate increased by about 30 degrees for strong partisans. During the same period, the average difference increased by about 10 degrees for weak and independent partisans and was unchanged for pure independents. These results support the conclusion that strong partisans now perceive a much greater stake in the outcomes of elections than they did in the past while weak and independent partisans perceive a somewhat larger stake and pure independents perceive no larger a stake than in the past.

The Changing Partisan Composition of the Electorate

The turnout trends displayed in Figure 5.1 have had important consequences for the partisan composition of the American electorate. The results can be seen in Figure 5.3, which displays the partisan composition of the 2004 electorate based on ANES data. Because of the exceptionally high turnout rate of strong partisans and the exceptionally low turnout rate of pure independents, strong partisans are overrepresented in the contemporary electorate, and pure independents are underrepresented. In 2004, according to the ANES data, strong partisans made up about 40 percent of the electorate, and pure independents made up only 5 percent of the electorate.

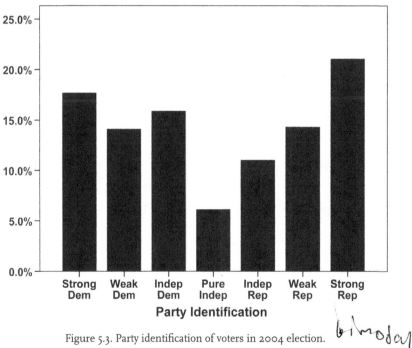

Figure 5.3. Party identification of voters in 2004 election.
(*Source:* 2004 American National Election Study.)

The data displayed in Figure 5.3 reflect another important feature of the contemporary American electorate—the close balance of support between the two major parties. According to the ANES data, Democratic identifiers and leaners and Republican identifiers and leaners both composed about 47 percent of the electorate in 2004. These results are similar to those from other national surveys and from the 2004 NEP. According to that poll, Republicans made up about 37 percent of the electorate, Democrats about 37 percent, and independents about 26 percent. (The proportion of independents was much larger in the NEP sample than in the ANES sample because NEP surveys do not ask independents whether they lean toward one party or another.) The results are also similar to those from various national surveys conducted at the time of the 2006 midterm election and the 2008 presidential election although these more recent surveys have generally found a modest Democratic advantage in party identification. In the 2006

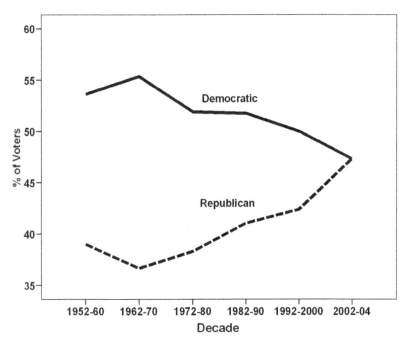

Figure 5.4. Party identification of voters by decade.
(*Source:* American National Election Studies.)

NEP, Democratic identifiers made up 38 percent of the electorate, Republican identifiers 35 percent, and independents 27 percent; in the 2008 NEP, Democratic identifiers made up 39 percent of the electorate, Republican identifiers 32 percent, and independents 29 percent.

The close balance between Democrats and Republicans in the contemporary electorate represents a dramatic change from the situation that existed for several decades following the end of World War II. During those years, Democratic identifiers and leaners typically outnumbered Republican identifiers and leaners by a wide margin.[7] Figure 5.4 displays the trends in the proportions of voters identifying with or leaning toward the Democratic and Republican parties in ANES surveys from the 1950s through the first decade of the twenty-first century. According to these data, Democrats enjoyed a 15- to 20-point advantage in voter identification during the 1950s and 1960s. Since that time, however, the Democratic advantage has been shrinking steadily, and by 2002–2004, the Democratic advantage in voter identification had disappeared.

Ideological Realignment and Its Consequences

Since the 1970s, and perhaps earlier, an ideological realignment has been occurring within the American electorate—one that reflects the realignment occurring among political elites. Figure 5.5 shows that since the 1970s, when the ANES started asking an ideological identification question, conservative voters have been moving steadily away from the Democratic Party and toward the Republican Party while moderate-to-liberal voters have been moving steadily, although less dramatically, toward the Democratic Party and away from the Republican Party. In the overall electorate, the percentage of conservative voters identifying with or leaning toward the Democratic Party declined by 17 points between the 1970s and the first decade of the twenty-first century. During the same period, the percentage of moderate-to-liberal voters identifying with or leaning toward the Democratic Party increased by 9 points.

Between the 1970s and the beginning of the twenty-first century, ideological realignment eliminated the Democratic Party's traditional advantage in voter identification. This is because the movement of conservatives into

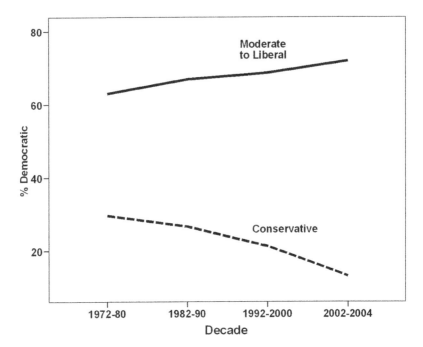

Figure 5.5. Trend in Democratic identification of voters by ideology.
(*Source:* American National Election Studies.)

the Republican camp during this period greatly exceeded that of moderates and liberals into the Democratic camp. But this movement now appears to be largely complete; there are relatively few conservative Democrats left to realign. In fact, since 2004 Democratic identification has been increasing, especially among younger Americans. And although ideological realignment has left the Democratic Party with a smaller electoral base, it has also left it with a more loyal one. As Figure 5.6 shows, the average rate of loyalty in presidential voting among Democratic identifiers and leaners has increased dramatically since the 1970s.

   During the 1970s, Democratic identifiers and leaners were three times as likely to defect to the opposing party's presidential candidates as Republican identifiers and leaners. Since 1992, however, Democratic identifiers and leaners have been just as loyal, if not more loyal, to their party's presidential candidates as Republican identifiers and leaners. The explanation

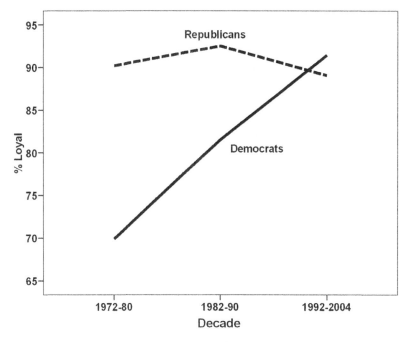

Figure 5.6. Party loyalty in presidential voting by decade.
(*Source:* American National Election Studies.)

for this change, of course, is that the conservatives, who were by far the least loyal Democrats, have largely moved into the Republican camp. As a result, we are left with two parties that are closely matched in both size and voter loyalty.

Partisan voting patterns in the 2004 presidential and congressional elections clearly reflected these trends. The rates of party loyalty among both Democrats and Republicans were very high. According to data from the 2004 ANES, 91 percent of Democratic identifiers and leaners and 92 percent of Republican identifiers and leaners voted for their party's presidential candidate, and 86 percent of Democratic identifiers and leaners and 82 percent of Republican identifiers and leaners voted for their party's U.S. House candidate. Rates of party loyalty were just as high or higher in the 2004 NEP. In that survey, of more than thirteen thousand voters leaving their polling places, 89 percent of Democratic identifiers and 94 percent of

Republican identifiers voted for the party's presidential candidate, and 91 percent of Democratic identifiers and 93 percent of Republican identifiers voted for their party's U.S. House candidate.

In the 2006 midterm election, Democrats took control of both chambers of Congress for the first time in twelve years, gaining thirty seats in the House of Representatives and six in the Senate. Two years later Democrats won the presidency and gained an additional twenty-one House seats and eight Senate seats. But despite the dramatic change in the fortunes of the parties, the 2006 and 2008 elections resembled the 2004 election in one important respect: the high level of party loyalty displayed by the voters. According to the 2006 NEP, 93 percent of Democratic identifiers voted for a Democratic House candidate, and 93 percent voted for a Democratic Senate candidate. And Republican identifiers were almost as loyal: 92 percent voted for a Republican House candidate, and 86 percent voted for a Republican Senate candidate. Similarly, in 2008, according to the NEP, 89 percent of Democrats voted for Barack Obama, and 92 percent voted for a Democratic House candidate; while 90 percent of Republicans voted for John McCain, and 89 percent voted for a Republican House candidate.

The high levels of party loyalty displayed by Democratic and Republican identifiers in recent elections are a direct result of the ideological realignment that has occurred over the past several decades in the United States. Because of this realignment, there is a high level of partisan-ideological consistency in the contemporary electorate: there are far more liberal Democrats and conservative Republicans than conservative Democrats and liberal Republicans. Therefore, ideology is much more likely to reinforce party identification than to undermine it.[8] This can be seen in Table 5.1, which displays the relationship between partisan-ideological consistency and voting behavior in the 2004 presidential and U.S. House elections.

I measured partisan-ideological consistency among respondents in the 2004 ANES by comparing their party identification with their scores on a liberal-conservative policy scale. Democratic identifiers and leaners whose scores fell in the most liberal third of the policy scale and Republican identifiers and leaners whose scores fell in the most conservative third of the policy scale were classified as high on partisan-ideological consistency. Conversely, Democratic identifiers and leaners whose scores fell in the most

Table 5.1. Party loyalty in 2004 presidential and House elections
by partisan-ideological consistency

Partisan-ideological consistency	% of Identifiers	% Loyal in	
		Presidential election	House election
High	62	99	92
Moderate	30	84	76
Low	8	66	59

Source: 2004 American National Election Study.
Note: Based on all identifiers and leaners.

conservative third of the policy scale and Republican identifiers and leaners whose scores fell in the most liberal third of the policy scale were classified as low on partisan-ideological consistency. All party identifiers and leaners whose scores fell in the middle third of the policy scale were classified as moderate on partisan-ideological consistency.

Table 5.1 shows that 62 percent of all party identifiers and leaners who reported voting in the 2004 presidential election were classified as high on partisan-ideological consistency and only 8 percent as low. Moreover, there was a strong relationship between partisan-ideological consistency and party loyalty. In both the presidential and U.S. House elections, those who were classified as high on partisan-ideological consistency, meaning liberal Democrats and conservative Republicans, voted overwhelmingly for their party's candidates. In contrast, in both types of elections those who were classified as low on partisan-ideological consistency, that is, conservative Democrats and liberal Republicans, defected to the other party's candidates between 30 percent and 40 percent of the time. These results make it clear that the high rates of party loyalty in recent presidential and congressional elections are explained largely by the high level of consistency between party identification and ideology in the contemporary electorate.

Another sign of growing party loyalty among voters has been a substantial decline in the frequency of ticket splitting over the past thirty years. Fig-

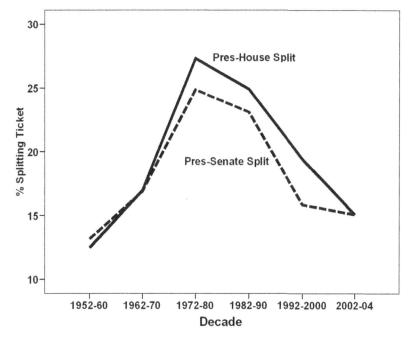

Figure 5.7. The rise and decline of ticket splitting.
(*Source:* American National Election Studies.)

ure 5.7 displays the trends in the frequency of ticket splitting between presidential and House voting and between presidential and Senate voting since
the 1950s based on ANES data. These data show that between the 1950s
and the 1970s the frequency of both types of ticket splitting almost doubled.
Since that time, however, the frequency of both types of ticket splitting has
been declining, and by 2004 the frequency had returned to about the levels
that prevailed during the 1950s.

This decline in ticket splitting can be traced directly to increasing partisan-
ideological consistency within the electorate. Individuals whose party identification and ideological orientation are consistent—liberal Democrats and
conservative Republicans—tend to vote more consistently across different
offices than individuals whose party identification and ideology are incon-
sistent—conservative Democrats and liberal Republicans. In 2004, for example, according to ANES data, the frequency of ticket splitting between

presidential and House voting ranged from 12 percent among voters who were classified as high on partisan-ideological consistency to 36 percent among voters who were classified as low.

Partisan-Ideological Polarization and Electoral Competition

Thus far we have seen that partisan-ideological polarization has had profound consequences for individual voting behavior, affecting turnout, party loyalty, and ticket splitting. But partisan-ideological polarization has also had important consequences for competition in presidential and congressional elections. The ideological realignment of the parties over the past several decades has produced a significant increase in geographical polarization. Conservative regions, states, and congressional districts have been trending toward the Republican Party while liberal regions, states, and congressional districts have been trending toward the Democratic Party.

The best-known example of ideological realignment at the regional level has been the movement of the once solidly Democratic South into the Republican camp over the past half century.[9] In both 2000 and 2004, George W. Bush captured all of the electoral votes from the eleven states of the old Confederacy, and despite suffering some losses in the 2006 midterm election, Republicans still held 77 of 131 House seats and 16 of 22 Senate seats from the region in the 110th Congress. Although Barack Obama made some inroads into the GOP's southern base in 2008—carrying Florida, North Carolina, and Virginia—most of the South remained loyal to the Republican Party even as the rest of the country was trending strongly in a Democratic direction. Outside of the South, the outcome of the 2008 presidential election was a Democratic landslide. John McCain won the popular vote in the South by about 9 points while losing it in the rest of the country by 17 points. McCain actually improved on Bush's 2004 margins in three southern states —Arkansas, Louisiana, and Tennessee. And although Democrats made some gains in the South during the 2008 congressional elections, Republicans continued to hold 15 of 22 southern Senate seats and 72 of 131 southern House seats in the 111th Congress.

But the South is not the only region of the country that has undergone a major transformation in its partisan loyalties since the end of World War II. The growing Republicanism of the South, the nation's most conservative region, has had its counterpart in the growing Democratic domination of the Northeast, the nation's most liberal region. Fifty years ago the Northeast constituted the heartland of the Republican Party. In 2004, however, John Kerry captured every electoral vote from the eleven northeastern states, and after the 2006 midterm election, Democrats held seventeen of the twenty-two Senate seats and sixty-eight of the ninety-two House seats from the region.[10] The 2008 election continued this trend. Barack Obama won every state in the Northeast by at least 10 points, and Democrats gained a Senate seat in New Hampshire and seven additional House seats. The defeat of Christopher Shays of Connecticut meant that for the first time since the Civil War, there would not be a single Republican in the House of Representatives from all of New England.

The 2000 and 2004 presidential elections were both extremely competitive at the national level. In 2000 George W. Bush won a disputed victory in the Electoral College despite losing the national popular vote to Al Gore by about half of a percentage point; in 2004 Bush won a second term as president after defeating John Kerry by a margin of less than 3 percentage points in the national popular vote. Bush's popular vote margin in 2004 was the smallest for a reelected incumbent in modern history.

But although these two presidential elections were extremely competitive at the national level, they were not very competitive in most of the states. Compared with the presidential elections of 1960 and 1976, which were also closely contested at the national level, there were far fewer battleground states in 2000 and 2004, and the percentage of electoral votes in these battleground states was much smaller. The average margin of victory at the state level has increased dramatically over time, and far more states with far more electoral votes are now either solidly Democratic or solidly Republican. In the 2004 presidential election, thirty-one states were carried by Bush or Kerry by a margin of more than 10 percentage points. These states included the large majority of the nation's voters, and they cast 332 of the 538 electoral votes. Only twelve states were decided by a margin of fewer than 5 percentage points. These twelve competitive states cast only 141 electoral votes, and they included only three large states: Florida, Ohio, and Pennsylvania. But these twelve states were the battleground on which the 2004 presidential election was fought. George Bush won two of them—Florida and Ohio. If John Kerry had carried either one, he would have become the forty-fourth president of the United States.

In 2008 Barack Obama won the national popular vote by a margin of just over 7 percentage points. His margin in the national popular vote would not be considered a landslide, but the Democratic ticket did carry many states by landslide or near-landslide margins, including several of the most populous ones. For example, Obama carried California by 24 points, New York by 25 points, Illinois by 25 points, Michigan by 16 points, and Pennsylvania by 10 points. Of the twenty-eight states carried by the Democratic ticket, the margin was greater than 10 points in twenty-one of them and less than 5 points in only four. And despite the decisive Democratic victory, many states that voted for the Republican ticket also did so by landslide or near-landslide margins. Of the twenty-two states carried by John McCain, the margin was greater than 10 points in fifteen of them and less than 5 points in only two. And although the nation as a whole was moving in a Democratic direction between 2004 and 2008, the Republicans managed to increase their margin of victory in four states: Oklahoma, Arkansas, Louisiana, and Tennessee.

A similar pattern was evident in the election results at the county level. According to an analysis by the *New York Times,* between 2004 and 2008 the Democratic share of the vote increased in 2,437 of the nation's 3,141 counties; at the same time, the Republican share increased in 678 counties. The Democratic share of the vote increased by more than 10 points in 1,173 counties, and the Republican share increased by more than 10 points in 225 counties. Counties with the largest increases in the Democratic share of the vote were generally found in large metropolitan areas with relatively high levels of education and large concentrations of Hispanic and African American voters. Counties with the largest increases in the Republican share of the vote were generally found in small towns and rural areas with relatively low levels of education, small minority populations, and high concentrations of Southern Baptists. Many of these Republican-tilting counties were located in the Appalachian region.

The overall picture that emerges from an examination of the 2008 electoral map is one of a country that had moved rather dramatically in a Democratic direction since 2004 but that remained deeply divided. Across all fifty states and the District of Columbia, the average margin of victory for the winning party increased from 15.8 points in 2004 to 17.4 points in 2008. There were more landslide and near-landslide states and fewer closely contested states. The number of states in which the winning candidate's margin of victory was greater than 10 points increased from thirty to thirty-five, and the number in which the winning candidate's margin of victory was fewer than 5 points decreased from eleven to six. Of the seven most populous states, only two—Florida and Ohio—were decided by fewer than 5 points, and three—New York, California, and Illinois—were decided by more than 20 points.

Although Barack Obama won a decisive victory in 2008, his support across states and regions of the country diverged widely. This pattern of geographical polarization is consistent with the pattern evident in other recent presidential elections, including the 2004 election, but it represents a dramatic change from the more homogeneous voting patterns that existed during the 1960s and 1970s. In the closely contested 1960 and 1976 elections, for example, there were far more closely contested states and far fewer landslide states than in recent presidential elections. And in both of those elections every one of the most populous states was closely contested, including California, New York, Illinois, and Texas. The divisions between red states and blue states are far deeper today than they were thirty or forty years ago, and the 2008 election did nothing to change that reality.

The decline in competition at the state level has been paralleled by a decline in competition in congressional elections. Just as more and more states are now safe for one party in presidential and Senate elections, more and more districts are now safe for one party in House elections.[11] House districts can be classified as safe for a party, favoring a party, or competitive on the basis of the normalized presidential vote in the district. When the Democratic or Republican presidential vote in a district is at least 10 percentage points more than the national Democratic or Republican presidential vote, that district can be considered safe for the winning party. Such districts rarely elect a representative from the minority party. In contrast, when the Democratic or Republican presidential vote in a district is within 5 percentage points of the national Democratic or Republican presidential vote, that district can be considered potentially competitive. Both parties have some chance of electing a representative from such a district, although the majority party in the district still generally has a significant advantage.

Between 1976 and 2004 the number of House districts classified as competitive based on the normalized presidential vote in the district fell from 187 to 103 while the number classified as safe for one party or the other rose from 122 to 216. Moreover, contrary to the claims of some scholars and journalists, the decline in the number of competitive House districts cannot be explained by the effects of partisan gerrymandering.[12] Reformers often cite the results of the 2001–2002 round of redistricting as demonstrating the worst abuses of partisan gerrymandering because of the extensive use of computerized databases and map-making programs in drawing new district lines.[13] However, an analysis of the evidence from this redistricting cycle shows not only that the proportions of safe and marginal districts changed very little between 2000 and 2002, but that who controlled redistricting had little or no effect on the proportions of safe and marginal districts. Regardless of whether there was one party control of redistricting, divided party control, or nonpartisan/judicial control, the proportions of safe and marginal districts changed little between 2000 and 2002. In fact, states in which redistricting was done by nonpartisan commissions or courts ended up with a slightly larger proportion of safe districts in 2002 (51 percent) than states in which redistricting was done by partisan legislatures (45 percent).

In general, redistricting had a minor effect on the competitiveness of House districts in each of the last three redistricting cycles. Instead, the most significant changes in the competitiveness of House districts occurred between redistricting cycles. This evidence is consistent with an ideological realignment hypothesis. As a result of population movement, immigration, and party realignment within the electorate, Republicans are increasingly surrounded by other Republicans and Democrats by other Democrats.[14] This trend has been evident since the 1970s, but it appears to have accelerated in recent years. Between 1992 and 2004, the number of marginal districts fell from 157 to 112 while the number of safe districts rose from 156 to 208.

The effect of this increase in partisan polarization has been magnified by the growing consistency of voting behavior between presidential and House elections. The correlation between the Democratic percentage of the House vote and the Democratic percentage of the presidential vote in House districts increased from .58 during the 1970s to .82 in 2002–2004. This was not simply a result of partisan realignment in the South: the same trend was evident in congressional districts outside of the South as well as those in the South. This growing consistency appears to reflect an increase in partisan voting in both presidential and congressional elections since the 1980s.[15]

As a result of both increased partisan polarization and increased partisan consistency in voting behavior, far fewer representatives now occupy high-risk districts (districts that are less supportive of their party than the national average), and far more representatives now occupy low-risk districts (districts that are at least 10 percentage points more supportive of their party than the national average). Since the 1970s, the percentage of Republicans in high-risk districts has fallen from 21.5 percent to 11.3 percent, and the percentage of Democrats in high-risk districts has fallen from 41.4 percent to 16.4 percent. At the same time, the percentage of Republicans in low-risk districts has risen from 23.2 percent to 40.8 percent, and the percentage of Democrats in low-risk districts has risen from 24.5 percent to 51.1 percent. Between 1972 and 2004, the total number of representatives representing high-risk districts fell from 157 to 97 while the total number representing low-risk districts rose from 50 to 203.

The changing partisan composition of House districts has important implications for competition in House elections. Compared with thirty years ago, a much smaller proportion of House members now represent districts that, based on presidential voting patterns, favor the opposing party: fewer Republicans represent Democratic-leaning districts, and far fewer Democrats represent Republican-leaning districts. These high-risk districts account for a disproportionate share of incumbent defeats and party turnover in House elections. For example, in the 1994 midterm election, in which Republicans regained control of the House of Representatives for the first time in forty years, 32 percent of Democratic incumbents in high-risk districts were defeated compared with only 7 percent of Democratic incumbents in all other districts. Only 34 percent of Democratic seats in 1994 were in high-risk districts, but 70 percent of Democratic seat losses occurred in these districts.

Compared with the 1970s and 1980s, a much larger proportion of House members now represent districts that, based on presidential voting patterns, strongly favor their own party: more Republicans represent solidly Republican districts, and more Democrats represent solidly Democratic districts. These low-risk districts account for a disproportionate share of uncontested and one-sided races. Even under the most unfavorable circumstances, incumbents in such districts are rarely defeated. For example, in the 1994 election, in which Republicans defeated more than thirty Democratic incumbents and took control of the House of Representatives, not one of the sixty-nine Democratic incumbents in a low-risk district was defeated.

A similar pattern was evident in the 2006 midterm election, in which Democrats regained control of both chambers of Congress for the first time since 1995. Republicans lost 59 percent of their seats in House districts in which George Bush had received less than 50 percent of the vote in 2004, 22 percent of their seats in districts in which Bush had received between 50 and 55 percent of the vote in 2004, and only 6 percent of their seats in districts in which Bush had received more than 55 percent of the vote in 2004. As a result, Republicans lost eleven of their thirty-one House seats in the Northeast but only two of their eighty-four House seats in the South. Thus, although Republicans suffered losses in all regions in 2006, the election results increased regional disparities in the strength of the parties, leaving Republicans in a relatively strong position in the South but even weaker in the Northeast than they had been previously.

In the Senate as well, Democratic gains in 2006 occurred disproportionately in states that Bush had lost or won by a relatively narrow margin in 2004. Republicans lost five of their seven Senate seats in states in which Bush received less than 55 percent of the vote in 2004 but only one of their eight seats in states in which he received more than 55 percent of the vote in 2004. And in the Senate, as in the House, the fact that Republican losses occurred disproportionately in Democratic or marginally Republican states resulted in an increase in regional disparities in party strength. Republicans lost four of six seats in the Northeast and Midwest but only two of nine seats in the South and West. In the 110th Congress, Republicans were left with only five Senate seats from the eleven northeastern states.

Partisan-Ideological Polarization and Political Campaigns

Increasing party loyalty in voting and increasing one-party dominance of many states and congressional districts have contributed to changes in the campaign strategies of the candidates and parties. The primary emphasis in most political campaigns today is not on persuading swing voters but on mobilizing core party supporters. This shift in emphasis has important implications for many aspects of campaign strategy, including resource allocation, voter targeting, and message content.

Political campaigns generally have two major goals: persuading swing voters, true independents, and weak supporters of the opposing party, and mobilizing core party supporters.[16] The relative importance of these two goals depends primarily on the partisan composition of the electorate in a state or district. In a state or district in which one party enjoys a dominant position, the candidate of the dominant party can generally win simply by mobilizing his or her party's core supporters. There is little need to bother appealing to swing voters or supporters of the opposing party, and indeed, such appeals could alienate core party supporters and potentially encourage a primary challenge. Minority party candidates in states or districts dominated by the opposing party generally lack the visibility and financial resources to conduct meaningful campaigns. With minimal resources and little or no chance of winning, such candidates frequently confine themselves to appealing to their own party's core supporters.

We have seen that over the past thirty years the proportion of states and congressional districts in which one party enjoys a dominant position has increased substantially. As a result, most House campaigns and many Senate campaigns today are more concerned with mobilizing core party supporters than with appealing to swing voters. The main emphasis in such campaigns is identifying and turning out voters who have been identified as supporters of the majority party, and campaign messages generally stress traditional party positions that appeal to these core party supporters.

In the minority of states or districts in which the party balance is relatively close, campaigns must attempt to appeal to swing voters while simultaneously attempting to mobilize core party supporters. Especially if both major party candidates possess adequate financial resources, this generally involves using television advertising to target swing voters with messages emphasizing personal qualities and issue positions with broad electoral appeal while using mailings and radio advertising to target core party supporters with messages stressing more traditional party positions. Even in these potentially competitive states and districts, however, because of increased partisan-ideological consistency and party loyalty, there are fewer swing voters to persuade than in the past. As a result, party organizations and candidates have been devoting more of their resources to grassroots voter registration and get-out-the-vote (GOTV) campaigns aimed at core party supporters.[17]

Evidence of this shift in emphasis can be seen in the 2004 Democratic and Republican presidential campaigns. The Bush and Kerry campaigns along with state and national party organizations and various allied groups devoted enormous resources to voter registration and GOTV efforts in the swing states. Donald Green, one of the nation's leading experts on GOTV campaigns,[18] recently estimated that spending by the presidential candidates and affiliated groups on mobilization efforts in battleground states tripled between 2000 and 2004, going from approximately $150 million to approximately $450 million.[19]

During the final days of the 2004 presidential campaign, the Republican Party implemented its vaunted "72-hour program" in key states such as Ohio, Florida, and Pennsylvania. This was a carefully planned effort to use individuals identified as supporters in heavily Republican neighborhoods and evangelical churches to contact their neighbors and fellow church members and urge them to turn out and vote for President Bush. Meanwhile, Democrats and their allies, including labor unions and "527" organizations such as Americans Coming Together, poured resources into more conventional GOTV efforts using paid canvassers to contact registered voters in heavily Democratic neighborhoods in the same states.

The Republican 72-hour program was widely credited with giving President Bush and other GOP candidates a decisive edge in the battleground states,[20] but the evidence from the 2004 election results indicates that both parties' mobilization efforts in these states were highly successful. Although voter turnout increased across the entire country in 2004, the largest increases occurred in the swing states. In Florida, for example, according to data compiled by Michael McDonald of George Mason University, turnout increased from 56 percent of eligible voters in 2000 to 65 percent in 2004. Similarly, in Ohio, turnout increased from 57 percent of eligible voters in 2000 to 67 percent in 2004; in Pennsylvania, it increased from 54 percent of eligible voters in 2000 to 62 percent in 2004.[21] And turnout increased substantially in both strongly Democratic and strongly Republican counties in these states. In Ohio, for example, the number of votes cast in the presidential election increased by 17 percent in strongly Democratic Cuyahoga County and by 22 percent in strongly Republican Butler County. In Ohio as a whole, the number of Republican votes increased by an impressive 21.7 percent between 2000 and 2004, but the number of Democratic votes increased by an even more impressive 25.4 percent.

Evidence from the 2004 ANES also shows that the voter mobilization efforts undertaken by both major parties were quite successful. Thirty-one percent of respondents interviewed after the 2004 election reported being contacted by the Democratic Party, shattering the previous record of 22 percent set in 2000. Twenty-eight percent of respondents reported being contacted by the Republican Party, also breaking the record of 25 percent set in 2000. In addition, 18 percent of voters reported being contacted before the election by a nonparty group or organization. These voter mobilization efforts continued in the 2008 campaign. According to the ANES, a record 32 percent of respondents reported being contacted by the Democratic Party; the 24 percent who reported being contacted by the Republican Party and the 17 percent reported being contacted by a nonparty group or organization were slightly below the levels of 2004 but well above the average levels for presidential elections since the 1950s.

Previous general election spending records were shattered by the presidential candidates and party organizations in 2008. According to figures compiled by the Campaign Finance Institute, between September 1 and October 15 the Obama campaign and the Democratic National Committee spent more than $266 million while the McCain campaign and the Republican National Committee spent more than $176 million. A good deal of this money was spent on television ads aimed at undecided voters, but both presidential campaigns also devoted substantial resources to voter registration and GOTV efforts in the battleground states. However, the Obama campaign had two crucial advantages over the McCain campaign when it came to voter mobilization: money and enthusiasm—and it put both of these advantages to good use.[22]

Because of the enormous success of its fund-raising operation, the Obama campaign was able to open dozens of field offices and send hundreds of paid organizers into every one of the major battleground states, including Florida, Ohio, Pennsylvania, Virginia, Indiana, and North Carolina. The size of the Obama field operation was unprecedented in the history of modern political campaigns. In most of the battleground states the number of Obama field offices greatly exceeded the number of McCain field offices. According to a count by Nate Silver of fivethirtyeight.com, as of August 9, 2008, the Obama campaign had opened 336 field offices in battleground states compared with only 101 for the McCain campaign; and unlike the Obama offices, many of the McCain field offices were actually being staffed by local Republican Party organizations. Obama field offices outnumbered McCain field offices by 33 to 9 in Ohio, 28 to 6 in Virginia, 27 to 7 in Missouri, and 14 to 3 in New Hampshire. In fact, Florida was the only state where McCain field offices outnumbered those of Obama (35 to 25).[23]

The other major advantage that the Obama campaign enjoyed when it came to voter mobilization was the much greater level of enthusiasm among Obama's supporters. This allowed the campaign to leverage its investment in campaign offices and paid staffers into an army of volunteers who could conduct voter registration and GOTV drives. Preliminary evidence indicates that this advantage in personnel allowed the Obama campaign to contact a larger proportion of the electorate than the McCain campaign in many of the key battleground states. According to data from state exit polls and compiled by Nate Silver,[24] the percentage of voters reporting contact by the Obama campaign exceeded the proportion reporting contact by the McCain campaign in eleven key battleground states. The largest gap was in Nevada, where 50 percent of voters reported contact by the Obama campaign versus 29 percent who reported contact by the McCain campaign. There were also double-digit contact gaps in favor of Obama in Colorado, Indiana, Virginia, Pennsylvania, and Iowa and smaller gaps in favor of Obama in Florida, North Carolina, Missouri, Ohio, and Wisconsin. Although it is impossible to measure the effect of voter mobilization efforts on the election results, it is probably not a coincidence that Obama ended up carrying all of these battleground states except Missouri. In an electorate characterized by strong party loyalties and politically homogeneous communities, mobilizing core party supporters can be a more efficient use of scarce campaign resources than trying to persuade swing voters.[25]

Partisan-Ideological Polarization and Primary Elections

In the growing number of states and congressional districts dominated by one party, primary elections play a crucial role in the selection of political leaders. But a recent study of primary elections in the United States found that competition in primaries has been declining since the early twentieth century and that incumbent officeholders now rarely face serious primary opposition.[26] There are a number of reasons why this is so, including the enormous financial advantage that incumbents typically enjoy. However, one important factor in the decline of primary competition in recent years may be partisan-ideological polarization.

When there were serious ideological divisions within the Democratic and Republican parties, ideological factionalism was an important source of competition in primaries.[27] Moderate-to-liberal Republicans might find themselves challenged by conservatives, and moderate-to-conservative Democrats might find themselves challenged by liberals. As recently as 1976, Republican president Gerald Ford, who was generally considered a moderate conservative, found himself challenged for his party's presidential nomination by Ronald Reagan, the leader of the conservative faction within the Republican Party. Four years later, President Jimmy Carter, a moderate southern Democrat, faced a serious challenge from Edward Kennedy, the most visible leader of the liberal wing of the Democratic Party. But today, the ideological divisions within both major parties are much more muted. Barring a scandal, unless an incumbent's voting record is clearly outside of the ideological mainstream of his or her party, a serious primary challenge is unlikely.

Primary competition is generally much more vigorous when an open seat exists, as was the case in the 2008 presidential race. Even then, however, ideological differences among the candidates within a party tend to be fairly minor. Some policy differences did emerge among the Republican presidential contenders in 2008, with former Massachusetts governor Mitt Romney and former Arkansas governor Mike Huckabee both attempting to run against Arizona senator John McCain from the right. However, the most important differences among the candidates in both parties involved their backgrounds, qualifications, and personalities.[28] All of the major Democratic candidates ran as strong opponents of the war in Iraq and strong supporters of government-sponsored universal health care. Likewise, all of the major Republican candidates ran as strong supporters of the war and strong opponents of any major expansion of the federal role in health care.

Ideology and issue positions played a relatively minor role in voter decision making in the 2008 Democratic and Republican presidential primaries, and this situation is fairly typical for contested Democratic and Republican primaries in recent years. The serious Republican candidates in these competitive primaries are almost all conservatives of one stripe or another, and the serious Democratic candidates are almost all liberals.

Chapter Summary

Almost every aspect of the electoral process in the United States has been affected by the growth of partisan-ideological polarization over the past forty years. The large majority of voters are aligned with one of the two major parties, and party loyalty in voting is very high. Ticket splitting has been declining, and election outcomes increasingly reflect the relative strength of the parties in a constituency. With the large majority of House districts and states clearly favoring one party or the other, control of Congress and the presidency now hinges on a relatively small set of competitive districts and states. In these swing states and districts, the electoral battle is intense, with both parties pouring resources into television ads targeting swing voters and, increasingly, into voter registration and GOTV campaigns aimed at maximizing turnout of core party supporters.

The number and identity of these battleground states and districts varies depending on the national political climate. When there is a strong national tide favoring one party, as was the case in the 2006 midterm election, and again in the 2008 presidential and congressional elections, the number of states and districts in play can increase and the party that is in disfavor may be forced to fight the election on its home turf—defending states and districts that it normally counts on winning. Thus, in 2006, with public opinion running strongly against the Republican Party as a result of the unpopularity of President Bush and the war in Iraq, the number of House and Senate seats in play increased compared with other recent elections, and almost all of the competitive races were in districts and states previously held by Republicans.

Partisan-ideological realignment has not eliminated national tides in elections. It has, however, reduced their magnitude. The Democratic gains of thirty seats in the House of Representatives and six seats in the Senate in 2006 were the largest seat swings since the Republican takeover of both chambers in the 1994 midterm elections. By historical standards, however, they were not very large. Seat swings of more than one hundred House seats occurred on several occasions during the nineteenth century, and swings of more than fifty House seats and ten Senate seats were fairly common during the first half of the twentieth century. But swings of this magnitude are now highly unlikely because so many House districts and states are safe for one party or the other.

In addition to national tides that temporarily benefit one party, the relative strength of the two major parties can be affected by longer term trends that benefit one party at the expense of the other. The current relatively even division of the electorate between the parties is not set in stone. In fact, there is evidence from polling data of a modest shift in the balance of party identification in favor of the Democratic Party since 2004 as a result of growing disillusionment with the Bush administration's conduct of the war in Iraq and management of the economy. This shift seems to have been concentrated among younger voters who were already disproportionately Democratic in their party loyalties. From a longer term perspective, however, what may be even more significant than this emerging generation gap are demographic trends such as declining marriage rates and increasing racial, ethnic, and religious diversity, which appear to be benefiting the Democratic Party.[29] I now turn to these trends and how they may affect the party system and electoral process.

6

Polarization in a Changing Electorate

IN 2008, FOR THE FIRST TIME since 1952, neither the incumbent president nor the incumbent vice president was a candidate for the presidency. And for the first time in twenty-four years, the United States did not have a presidential candidate named Bush or Clinton on the ballot. The Democratic and Republican candidates for president, Barack Obama and John McCain, promised to campaign in states that had not supported their party in recent presidential elections and to reach out to voters who have traditionally supported the opposing party.[1] And both Obama and McCain repeatedly emphasized their desire to reach across the aisle and work with members of the opposing party in order to end partisan gridlock in Washington. Obama, in particular, made reducing partisan rancor and changing the way Washington works an integral part of his campaign message.

These developments led to widespread speculation that an Obama presidency could lead to some moderation of the intense partisan conflict that has characterized American politics in recent years. With the end of the Bush administration, according to this reasoning, it might be possible to achieve some degree of bipartisan cooperation on the important issues facing the country. It was an appealing argument. But even if candidate Obama was sincere about his desire to reduce partisan conflict and work with the opposition party, the evidence presented in this book suggests that it will be very difficult if not impossible for President Obama to achieve this objective. That is because partisan conflict in Washington is not caused primarily by personal animosity between Democratic and Republican leaders but by partisan-ideological polarization.

The main reason it is so hard for Democrats and Republicans in Washington to cooperate is not that they don't like each other, but that they disagree profoundly about the major issues facing the country, as do their politically engaged supporters in the electorate. This reality is unlikely to change just because there is a new president in the White House. In fact, the policy differences between the presidential candidates and their supporters in 2008 were as great, if not greater, than at any time in recent history. Moreover, as I demonstrate in this chapter, certain long-term demographic trends, such as the growing proportion of college graduates in the population, are likely to produce an increase in partisan-ideological polarization in the future.

Political Engagement in 2008 and Beyond

We have seen that the level of political engagement in the American electorate set a modern record in 2004. With the Democratic and Republican presidential candidates taking diametrically opposing positions on almost every major domestic and foreign policy issue and with the two major parties and their interest group allies spending record amounts of money on voter registration and GOTV drives, turnout increased dramatically in almost every demographic category, reaching levels not seen since the 1960s. But it wasn't just voter turnout that increased in 2004. Almost every form of electoral participation increased. More Americans than ever talked to their friends and relatives about the election, displayed yard signs and bumper stickers, and contributed money to the parties and candidates.

Every available indicator of public interest and involvement indicates that the level of engagement in the 2008 election was even greater than it was in 2004. During the primary season, public opinion polls found interest in the 2008 presidential campaign to be substantially higher than it was at a comparable time during the 2004 or 2000 campaigns. In a Gallup Poll conducted between January 29 and February 2, 2008, for example, 71 percent of respondents stated that they were giving "quite a lot" of thought to the presidential election. Four years earlier, in early February 2004, only 58 percent of respondents said the same thing; and four years before that, in January 2000, that number was only 38 percent.[2]

Another indicator of political engagement, participation in the presidential primaries and caucuses, provided an early indication that 2008 would be a record-setting year for voter turnout and other campaign-related activities. In almost every state, turnout in the primaries and caucuses, especially on the Democratic side, was considerably higher than it was four years or eight years before. In New Hampshire, for example, turnout in the Democratic primary increased from 147,000 in 2000 to 217,000 in 2004 and 284,000 in 2008. In South Carolina, which did not hold a primary in 2000, turnout increased from 291,000 in 2004 to 530,000 in 2008. Some 57 million voters participated in the Democratic and Republican primaries in 2008 compared with about 33 million in 2000, which was the last time both parties had contested nomination races. Participation in Democratic primaries increased from about 14 million in 2000 and 16 million in 2004 to about 38 million in 2008.

Interest and participation in the Democratic primaries and caucuses were driven in part by a prolonged and competitive nomination race between two pathbreaking candidates, Barack Obama and New York senator and former first lady Hillary Clinton. The Democratic candidates, and especially Obama, also had record numbers of individuals contribute to their campaigns, mainly via the Internet. According to data compiled by the Campaign Finance Institute, through April of 2008 Obama raised a record $263 million, of which almost $124 million came from individuals giving less than $200. During the same period, Hillary Clinton raised $198 million, of which more than $65 million came from individuals giving less than $200.[3]

Interest and participation were not as high on the Republican side where John McCain clinched the nomination relatively early. About 20 million voters participated in Republican presidential primaries in 2008, which was only a slight increase from the 19 million who participated in 2000. And the McCain campaign did not receive nearly as many individual contributions as the Obama and Clinton campaigns. According to the Campaign Finance Institute, through April 2008 McCain had raised $97 million, of which more than $22 million came from individuals giving less than $200. Nevertheless, spurred on by McCain's selection of Sarah Palin as his running mate and fear of what an Obama presidency might mean for the direction of the country, Republicans turned out in large numbers in the general election. Almost 132 million Americans voted in the 2008 presidential election, representing almost 62 percent of the nation's eligible voters, the highest turnout in forty years.[4]

Although the candidacies of Barack Obama and Hillary Clinton along with the intensity of the Democratic nomination battle clearly contributed to public interest and participation in the 2008 presidential election, the fundamental force driving political engagement in 2008, as in 2004, was partisan-ideological polarization. Notwithstanding John McCain's reputation as a maverick and the relatively moderate voting record that he compiled during most of his years in the Senate, the 2008 presidential election presented voters with a clear ideological choice.

On almost every major national issue—taxes, economic policy, national security, foreign policy, health care, education, energy, the environment, and abortion—the differences between the candidates were stark.[5] McCain proposed making the Bush tax cuts permanent; Obama proposed ending them and replacing them with tax cuts for low- to moderate-income families. Although both McCain and Obama eventually supported the Bush administration's $700 billion bailout plan to rescue financial institutions caught up in the subprime mortgage crisis, McCain opposed forcing banks to renegotiate the terms of these mortgages; Obama favored using bankruptcy courts to assist homeowners threatened with foreclosure. McCain consistently supported the war in Iraq and the Bush troop surge; Obama consistently opposed them. McCain proposed addressing the problem of the growing number of Americans without health insurance through tax incentives and high-deductible private insurance plans; Obama proposed making government-sponsored insurance available to all Americans, with subsidies to low-income citizens. McCain called for ending a federal moratorium on offshore oil drilling along the U.S. coastline; Obama opposed any expanded oil exploration in environmentally sensitive areas. McCain supported a wide variety of restrictions on access to abortion; Obama consistently opposed such restrictions.

To quantify the magnitude of the policy differences between these two presidential candidates, we can compare the ratings given to them by several prominent liberal organizations based on their recent voting records. In 2006 Barack Obama received a rating of 95 out of 100 from the liberal Americans for Democratic Action (as did Hillary Clinton); John McCain re-

POLARIZATION IN A CHANGING ELECTORATE

ceived a rating of 15. Obama received a rating of 100 from the National Abortion Rights Action League; McCain received a rating of 0. Obama received a rating of 100 from the National Education Association; McCain received a rating of 0. And Obama received a rating of 93 from the American Federation of Labor and Congress of Industrial Organizations (AFL-CIO); McCain received a rating of 7.[6]

With Democrats almost certain to control both the House and Senate in 2009, it was clear to voters that the policy consequences of a Democratic victory in the 2008 presidential election would be enormous. Unified Democratic control of Congress and the White House would result in major changes in almost every area of domestic and foreign policy. For both Democratic and Republican voters, therefore, the stakes in the 2008 presidential election were as large as they had been in any election during the past half century. It is hardly surprising, therefore, that the level of interest and participation in 2008 was extraordinarily high.

The results of the 2008 NEP indicate that while Barack Obama ran ahead of John Kerry in almost every demographic group, the voting patterns were very similar to those from four years earlier. According to the NEP, Obama won 56 percent of the vote among women but only 49 percent among men. The 7-point gender gap was identical to the gender gap in the 2004 NEP. McCain received 74 percent of the vote among whites who described themselves as born-again or evangelical Christians. This was only slightly smaller than George Bush's 77 percent vote share among this group in the 2004 NEP. Even with regard to race, the patterns of support in 2008 were very similar to those in 2004. Obama won 95 percent of the vote among African Americans but only 43 percent of the vote among whites. The 52-point racial divide was even larger than the 47-point divide in the 2004 NEP.

No Democratic presidential candidate since Lyndon Johnson has won a majority of the white vote, so the fact that Barack Obama lost the white vote was hardly surprising. Obama's 12-point deficit among white voters was identical to that of Al Gore in 2000. However, the fact that white voters favored the Republican presidential candidate by a double-digit margin in 2008 despite the poor condition of the economy and the extraordinary unpopularity of the incumbent Republican president suggests that racial prejudice did affect the level of white support for the Democratic candidate.

Further evidence of the effects of race can be seen in state exit poll results. White support for Obama varied dramatically across regions and states, ranging from a low of around 10 percent in the Deep South to close to 60 percent in parts of the Northeast and West. In many states outside the South, Obama did substantially better than Kerry among white voters. Between 2004 and 2008 the Democratic share of the white vote increased by 5 points in California and Washington, 7 points in Michigan and Wisconsin, 8 points in Colorado, and 9 points in Oregon. In some southern and border South states, however, Obama did no better or worse than Kerry among white voters. Between 2004 and 2008 the Democratic share of the white vote fell by 4 points in Mississippi, 6 points in Arkansas, 9 points in Alabama, and 10 points in Louisiana.

On the basis of these results, it is hard to avoid the conclusion that racial prejudice was a factor in limiting support for Barack Obama among white voters in the southern and border South states. But this was not enough to cost him the election because his losses among these groups of white voters were offset by gains among white voters in other parts of the country, especially among younger white voters, and by increased turnout and support among African American and Hispanic voters.

According to the NEP data, Obama had a 36-point lead over McCain among Hispanic voters, much larger than Kerry's 10-point margin over Bush in 2004. But this may reflect a return to a more typical voting pattern for this group—Bush's performance among Hispanic voters in 2004 was unusually strong for a Republican. In addition, there was a much larger generation gap in 2008 than in 2004. Obama did far better than Kerry among voters younger than thirty but about the same as Kerry among those sixty-five and older. Obama had a 34-point lead among eighteen-to-twenty-nine-year-olds compared with Kerry's 9-point lead among this group. However, Obama's 8-point deficit among those sixty-five and older was almost identical to Kerry's 5-point deficit among seniors.

Geographical voting patterns in 2008 also showed a high degree of continuity: across all fifty states and the District of Columbia, the correlation between the partisan division of the vote in 2004 and the partisan division of the vote in 2008 was .94, which was only slightly lower than the .97 correlation between 2000 and 2004. The overall picture that emerges from an examination of the 2008 electoral map is one of a country that moved rather dramatically in a Democratic direction but remained deeply divided. The average margin of victory for the winning party increased from 15.8 points in 2004 to 17.4 points in 2008. There were more landslide and near-landslide states and fewer closely contested states. The number of states in which the winning candidate's margin of victory was greater than 10 points increased from thirty to thirty-five while the number in which that margin was less than 5 points decreased from eleven to six. Of the seven most populous states, only Florida and Ohio were decided by fewer than 5 points while New York, California, and Illinois were decided by more than 20 points.

Although Barack Obama won a decisive victory in 2008, his support across states and regions of the country diverged widely. He made inroads into the Republican Party's traditional southern base by carrying Virginia, North Carolina, and Florida, but John McCain carried the other eight states of the old Confederacy along with the border states of Kentucky, West Virginia, and Oklahoma, winning most of them by double-digit margins. Altogether, McCain won 54 percent of the vote in the South and border South, and Obama won 57 percent of the vote in the rest of the country.

The high level of geographical polarization in 2008 is consistent with the pattern evident in other recent presidential elections, including the 2004 election, but it represents a dramatic change from the more homogeneous voting patterns that existed during the 1960s and 1970s. In the closely contested 1960 and 1976 elections, for example, there were far more closely contested states and far fewer landslide states than in recent presidential elections. And in both of those elections every one of the most populous states was closely contested, including California, New York, Illinois, and Texas. The divisions between red states and blue states are far deeper today than they were thirty or forty years ago, and the 2008 election did nothing to change this reality.

Evidence of continuing partisan-ideological polarization in 2008 can be found in polling data on the political orientations of Obama and McCain supporters. For example, during the final two weeks before the election, the Gallup Poll found that Obama was leading McCain by 92 points among liberal Democrats while McCain was leading Obama by 88 points among conservative Republicans. Other partisan-ideological groupings fell in between the two polar

groups, with moderate Democrats supporting Obama by 82 points, conservative Democrats supporting Obama by 70 points, and moderate-to-liberal Republicans supporting McCain by 59 points. Pure independents split fairly
evenly, favoring McCain by 2 points. These data make clear that despite Barack
Obama's decisive victory, the partisan and ideological divisions in the country
were as deep or deeper in 2008 as in other recent elections.

Further evidence of sharp ideological differences between Obama and
McCain voters comes from a *Time* Magazine Poll conducted October 3–6,
just one month before the election. In this poll, Obama led McCain among
likely voters by 5 points, 48 percent to 43 percent, which was very close to his
7-point margin on Election Day. The poll included questions asking respondents to place themselves on a series of 11-point (0–10) issue scales in
addition to the standard party and ideological identification questions. The
issues included abortion, gay marriage, environmental protection, regulation of financial institutions, off-shore oil drilling, health insurance, and the
war in Iraq. Responses to these seven issue questions along with the ideological identification question can be combined to construct a political ideology scale with scores ranging from 0 (consistently conservative) to 100
(consistently liberal).[7]

The *Time* poll also included five political information questions asking
respondents to identify the home state of Barack Obama and to name the
people holding four major government offices: vice president, secretary of
the treasury, speaker of the House of Representatives, and chief justice of the
Supreme Court. Answers to these questions can be combined to construct
a political knowledge scale with scores ranging from 0 to 5.

Obama supporters were significantly more liberal than McCain supporters
on all seven policy issues, with the largest differences on the issues of Iraq,
health insurance, abortion, and gay marriage. For example, on the issue of
abortion, 68 percent of Obama supporters took a strongly prochoice position
(scale scores 8–10) compared with only 25 percent of McCain supporters.
Similarly, on the issue of health care, 67 percent of Obama supporters strongly

---

Figure 6.1. (Right) Ideology scores of Obama and McCain supporters by political
information. (*Source: Time* Magazine Poll, October 3–6, 2008.)

Low Information Voters

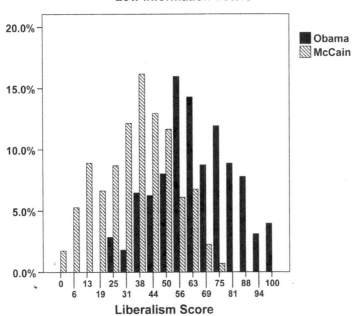

High Information Voters

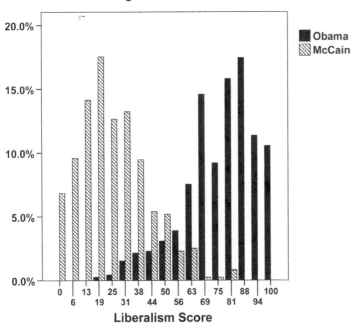

*high
Contrast*

favored a government-sponsored universal health insurance plan (scale scores 8–10) compared with only 11 percent of McCain supporters.

Obama and McCain supporters also differed dramatically in their overall ideological orientations. The vast majority of Obama supporters were found on the liberal side of our eight-item political ideology scale while the vast majority of McCain supporters were found on the conservative side. Among all likely voters the average liberalism score was 73 percent for Obama supporters versus 29 percent for McCain supporters. As we would expect, however, differences between Obama supporters and McCain supporters were substantially greater among informed than uninformed voters. This can be seen in Figure 6.1, which displays two distributions of Obama and McCain supporters on the ideology scale, one for low information voters (those with scores of 0–2) and one for moderate-to-high information voters (those with scores of 3–5).

The two distributions look very different. There is considerable overlap between the scores of Obama and McCain supporters among low information voters but very little overlap among moderate-to-high information voters. For the 36 percent of likely voters with political knowledge scores of 0–2, the average liberalism score was 64 percent for Obama supporters versus 36 percent for McCain supporters; for the 64 percent of likely voters with political knowledge scores of 3–5, the average liberalism score was 77 percent for Obama supporters versus 24 percent for McCain supporters. The difference was almost twice as large for the more knowledgeable group as for the less knowledgeable group. In 2008, as in other recent elections, we see a very high level of partisan-ideological polarization in the American electorate, with the highest level of polarization among the most politically engaged citizens.

Beyond 2008: How Demographic Trends Are Transforming the American Electorate

Rising Levels of Education

The special circumstances of the 2008 presidential contest, especially the nomination of the first African American presidential candidate and a deepening economic crisis, have tended to obscure certain long-term demographic trends that are transforming the American electorate. However, these trends have already had important consequences for the composition of the Democratic and Republican electoral coalitions and the strategies of party leaders and candidates, and their effects are likely to intensify over the next several election cycles.

One of the most important of these demographic trends is the continuing rise in education levels in the American population.[8] Data from ANES surveys displayed in Figure 6.2 show that over the past half century, the proportion of voting-age Americans with no college education has declined steadily, falling from more than 80 percent in the 1950s to less than 40 percent in 2002–2004. At the same time, the proportion of college graduates in the voting-age population has increased from less than 10 percent in the 1950s to about 30 percent in 2002–2004. Among those who reported vot-

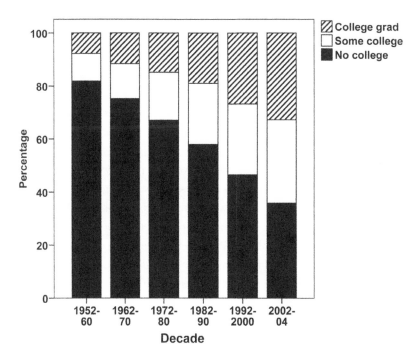

Figure 6.2. The changing educational composition of the voting-age population. (*Source:* American National Election Studies.)

ing in 2004, college graduates outnumbered those with no college education.

Data on generational differences in educational attainment indicate that the rise in education levels in the voting-age population has not yet run its course although future increases may be more gradual. Among respondents in the 2004 ANES, for example, only 23 percent of those older than sixty-five had graduated from college, compared with 31 percent of those younger than sixty-five; in contrast, 56 percent of respondents older than sixty-five had only a high school education, compared with only 35 percent of those younger than sixty-five. It is almost certain, therefore, that the proportion of college graduates in the voting-age population will continue to increase while the proportion with only a high school education will continue to decrease for the foreseeable future.

Rising levels of education are important because they can affect the level of engagement in the political process among citizens. College-educated citizens are generally more interested in politics, more politically active, and better informed about candidates and issues than high school–educated citizens. This is especially true with regard to one important form of political engagement: ideological awareness. Citizens with a college education generally display much higher levels of ideological awareness than those with a high school education. As a result, rising education levels have contributed to the growth of ideological awareness and sophistication in the American public over the past several decades.

Table 6.1 displays the trend since the 1970s in one key measure of ideological sophistication from ANES surveys: the percentage of respondents with different levels of education who were able to place themselves on the 7-point liberal-conservative scale and who perceived the Democratic Party as more liberal than the Republican Party. Being able to place oneself on a liberal-conservative scale and knowing the relative ideological positions of the two major parties are necessary conditions for achieving a high level of partisan-ideological consistency.

Table 6.1 shows that since the 1970s, the ideological sophistication of the American public has increased substantially. Over this period, the proportion of respondents able to place themselves on the 7-point liberal-conservative scale and aware of the difference between the parties' ideological po-

Table 6.1. Percentage of respondents able to place self on liberal-conservative
scale and aware of party difference by decade and education

	1972–1980	1982–1990	1992–2000	2002–2004
All respondents	40	45	50	63
Education				
High school	30	29	31	41
Some college	54	58	57	66
Graduate college	74	78	85	88

Source: American National Election Study Cumulative File.

sitions increased from 40 percent to 63 percent. A large part of the explanation for this increase in ideological sophistication was the rising level of
education in the populace. The evidence in the table shows that between the
1970s and the first decade of the twenty-first century, ideological sophistication increased within every educational category. However, during each
time period, the level of ideological sophistication was much higher than
average among college graduates and much lower than average among those
with only a high school education. Since the overall increase in ideological
sophistication was about twice as large as the average increase within each
educational category, we can conclude that about half of the overall increase
in ideological sophistication in the American public during these years was
due to rising levels of education.

By contributing to increased ideological sophistication, rising levels of education have been responsible for a large part of the increase in partisan-
ideological consistency in the American electorate over the past several
decades. Table 6.2 displays the relationship between ideological sophistication and partisan-ideological consistency in 2002–2004 among ANES respondents with varying levels of education. In this table, partisan-ideological consistency is measured by the correlation between the 7-point party
identification scale and the 7-point ideology scale: the stronger the correlation, the greater the degree of consistency.

The results in Table 6.2 show that the relationship between education and

Table 6.2. Partisan-ideological consistency
by ideological sophistication and education, 2002–2004

Education	Low sophistication	High sophistication
High school	.01	.64
Some college	.13	.69
Graduate college	.26	.80

Source: American National Election Study Cumulative File.
Note: Entries are Pearson product-moment correlations between 7-point liberal-conservative scale and 7-point party identification scale.

partisan-ideological consistency is largely mediated by ideological sophistication. Within each educational category, those who scored high on ideological sophistication were much more consistent than those who scored low. This means that the combined proportion of liberal Democrats and conservative Republicans was much higher in the high-sophistication groups than in the low-sophistication groups: liberal Democrats and conservative Republicans made up 58 percent of sophisticated respondents with a high school education, 67 percent of sophisticated respondents with some college education, and 75 percent of sophisticated college graduates; in contrast, liberal Democrats and conservative Republicans made up only 14 percent of unsophisticated respondents with a high school education, only 17 percent of unsophisticated respondents with some college education, and only 31 percent of unsophisticated college graduates.

By increasing the level of ideological sophistication in the public, rising levels of education have been an important factor in the growth of partisan-ideological consistency in the American electorate over the past several decades. Citizens with a college education are much more likely to understand ideological concepts and to use these concepts to evaluate the parties and candidates than citizens with only a high school education. As the level of education in the American population continues to increase, we can expect partisan-ideological consistency to continue to grow as well over the next several decades. Greater partisan-ideological consistency is likely to mean greater polarization and more intense partisan conflict in the future.

Along with greater partisan-ideological consistency, college graduates have more consistent beliefs across a wide range of issues than individuals with less formal education. In the 2004 ANES survey, respondents were asked for their positions on a variety of issues in addition to their ideological identification. These issues included abortion, gay marriage, gun control, health insurance, public versus private responsibility for jobs and living standards, government assistance to blacks, government spending and services, environmental protection, defense spending, and reliance on diplomacy versus military force in foreign policy. The average interitem correlation among these eleven items (the ten policy issues along with ideological identification) was .13 for respondents with a high school education, .28 for those with some college education, and .42 for college graduates.

Greater consistency across issues means greater ideological polarization because it means that opinions on different issues reinforce each other rather than canceling each other out. Those who are liberal on one issue tend to be liberal on other issues, and those who are conservative on one issue tend to be conservative on other issues. In order to demonstrate the significance of opinion consistency, I combined responses to the ten policy questions and the liberal-conservative identification question into an eleven-item liberal-conservative issues scale. The scale was then collapsed into six categories ranging from very liberal to very conservative. This collapsed scale was highly correlated with the presidential vote. Among respondents classified as "very liberal" or "liberal," only 7 percent voted for George Bush; among those classified as "leaning liberal," 36 percent voted for Bush; among those classified as "leaning conservative," 71 percent voted for Bush; and among those classified as "conservative" or "very conservative," 95 percent voted for Bush. These results indicate that the scale is a valid measure of ideological orientations in the electorate.

Figure 6.3 compares the distribution of opinion on the collapsed liberal-conservative issues scale among two groups of respondents: those with only a high school education and those who graduated from college. The results show that the opinions of college graduates were much more polarized than the opinions of those with only a high school education. Almost half of the

No College

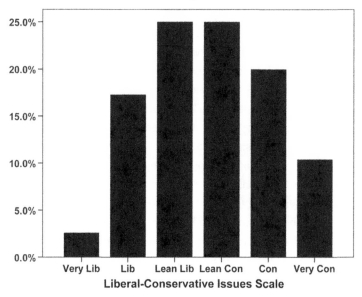

Liberal-Conservative Issues Scale

Graduated College

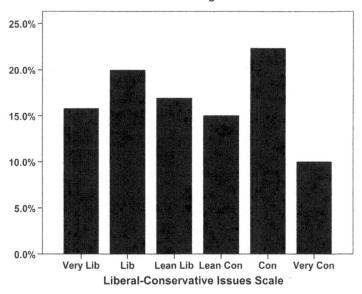

Liberal-Conservative Issues Scale

high school–educated respondents were located close to the center of the scale in the "lean liberal" or "lean conservative" categories; in contrast, less than one-third of the college graduates were located close to the center of the scale.

The fact that politically engaged citizens are drawn disproportionately from the ranks of college graduates helps to explain why partisan-ideological polarization is much greater among the politically engaged than among the politically disengaged. Among respondents in the 2004 ANES with a college degree, 65 percent engaged in at least one activity beyond voting, and the correlation between the liberal-conservative issues scale and party identification was .76; among those with only a high school education, only 43 percent engaged in at least one activity beyond voting, and the correlation between the liberal-conservative issues scale and party identification was only .51. These findings suggest that as education levels in the population continue to increase, we should expect both political engagement and partisan-ideological polarization to increase as well.

Race, Religion, and Marriage

As rising levels of education have been increasing the intensity of partisan-ideological polarization, other changes in American society have been altering the composition of both parties' electoral coalitions. Three long-term trends have been especially significant in this regard: increasing racial diversity, declining rates of marriage, and changes in religious beliefs. As a result of these trends, today's voters are less likely to be white, less likely to be married, and less likely to consider themselves Christians than voters of just a few decades ago. The combined effect of these trends on the composition of the electorate has been dramatic. Married white Christians now make up less than half of all voters in the United States and less than one-fifth of voters younger than thirty. The declining proportion of married white Christians in the electorate has important political implications because in recent years married white Christians have been among the most loyal sup-

Figure 6.3. (Left) Distribution on liberal-conservative issues scale by education in 2004. (*Source:* 2004 American National Election Study.)

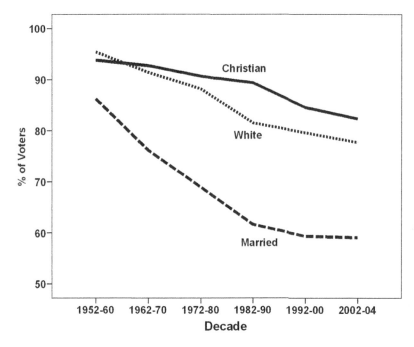

Figure 6.4. The changing social characteristics of the American electorate: race, religion, and marital status. (*Source:* American National Election Studies.)

porters of the Republican Party. In American politics today, whether one is a married white Christian is a much stronger predictor of one's political preferences than one's gender or class—the two demographic characteristics that dominate much of the debate on contemporary American politics.

Figure 6.4 displays the trends in the proportions of whites, married people, and Christian identifiers in the U.S. electorate over the past half century according to ANES data. Between the middle of the twentieth century and the beginning of the twenty-first, the proportion of whites has fallen by about 15 percentage points, the proportion of married people by about 25 percentage points, and the proportion of Christian identifiers by about 10 percentage points.

Married individuals still make up a large majority of the electorate, whites are still close to 80 percent of the electorate, and Christians still account for more than 80 percent of the electorate; however, the combined effect of the changes illustrated in Figure 6.4 has been enormous. Married white Christians have gone from close to 80 percent of the electorate in the 1950s to just over 40 percent in the first decade of the twenty-first century. Moreover, the decline in married white Christians has been even more drastic among younger voters. The proportion of married white Christians among voters younger than thirty has plummeted from almost 80 percent in the 1950s to less than 20 percent in the first decade of the twenty-first century. During the 1950s, 93 percent of voters younger than thirty were white; today, only 66 percent are white. During the 1950s, 95 percent of voters younger than thirty identified themselves as Christians; today, only 72 percent do. Finally and most dramatically, during the 1950s, 91 percent of voters younger than thirty were married; today, only 29 percent are married. The differences between younger and older voters today reflect a true generational shift, not just the normal consequences of aging.

These changes in the social composition of the American electorate are politically significant because married white Christians now constitute the core of the Republican electoral coalition. According to data from the 2006 NEP, Republican identifiers outnumbered Democratic identifiers by 49 percent to 26 percent among married white Christians; in contrast, Democratic identifiers outnumbered Republican identifiers by 48 percent to 24 percent among voters who were not married white Christians.

Not only are married white Christians much more likely to consider themselves Republicans than other Americans, but the percentage of married white Christians identifying with the Republican Party has increased substantially over the past several decades, going from about 40 percent in the 1960s to more than 60 percent in the first decade of the twenty-first century. Even though married white Christians have been shrinking as a proportion of the American electorate, the Republican Party has been able to maintain and even slightly increase its share of the electorate since the 1960s by steadily increasing its support among married white Christians. However, the ability of the GOP to continue to offset the diminishing size of its married white Christian base by making further gains among this group is now questionable.

Republican gains among married white Christians have occurred almost entirely among one segment of this group: self-identified conservatives. Between the 1970s and the first decade of the twenty-first century, Republican identification among conservative married white Christians increased by 26 points, going from 64 percent to 90 percent, according to ANES data. During the same period, Republican identification among moderate married white Christians increased by only 5 points, going from 38 percent to 43 percent, and Republican identification among liberal married white Christians actually declined by 10 points, falling from 23 percent to 13 percent. Thus, Republican gains among married white Christians have reflected the overall realignment of the American electorate along ideological lines over the past thirty to forty years, with conservatives increasingly identifying with the Republican Party and liberals increasingly identifying with the Democratic Party. These results suggest that the potential for additional Republican gains among married white Christians may be limited. Conservative married white Christians already overwhelmingly identify with the GOP, and the party has had little success in increasing its support among moderate-to-liberal married white Christians.

The danger posed to the Republican Party by the declining size of its married white Christian base was clearly illustrated by the results of the 2006 midterm election. According to the 2006 NEP, married white Christians made up just under half of the midterm electorate, and they voted for Republican over Democratic House candidates by a decisive 62 percent to 38 percent margin. However, voters who were not married white Christians made up just over half of the electorate, and they voted for Democratic over Republican House candidates by an even more decisive 68 percent to 32 percent margin. The result was a big win for the Democrats in the midterm election.

Demographic Change and the Generation Gap

In addition to the large gains Democrats made in the House and Senate elections, another striking feature of the 2006 results was the presence of a large generation gap within the electorate. As Table 6.3 shows, voters younger than thirty were considerably more likely to identify with the Democratic Party and vote for Democratic candidates than older voters. Although the youth vote was not solely responsible for the Democratic victory in 2006, the party's 22-point advantage among voters younger than thirty clearly contributed to the magnitude of that victory. That advantage only increased in

Table 6.3. The generation gap in 2006

	Age group		
	18–29 (%)	30–59 (%)	60+ (%)
Party identification			
Democratic	43	37	36
Independent	26	27	27
Republican	31	36	37
Ideology			
Liberal	34	20	15
Moderate	41	48	50
Conservative	25	32	35
House vote			
Democratic	61	54	51
Republican	39	46	49

Source: 2006 National Exit Poll.

2008 as Barack Obama trounced John McCain by a margin of 36 points among voters in this younger age group. And the Democratic advantage among younger voters was not confined to the presidential election: these voters favored Democratic candidates over Republican candidates for the House of Representatives by a 29-point margin.

An important question about the generation gap in recent elections is whether it was based mainly on short-term factors such as discontent with the war in Iraq and President Bush, or whether it reflected long-term trends in the demographic makeup of the American electorate. We have already seen that the decline in the proportion of married white Christians since the 1950s has been much more dramatic among younger voters than among older voters and the results of this long-term trend were clearly reflected in the social characteristics of the 2006 electorate. According to NEP data, only 17 percent of voters younger than thirty were married white Christians compared with more than half of older voters.

Table 6.4. Explaining the generation gap in political attitudes and behavior

	Age group			
	Married white Christians (%)		All others (%)	
	18–29	30+	18–29	30+
Party identification				
Democratic	26	26	47	49
Independent	22	24	28	28
Republican	53	49	26	23
Ideology				
Liberal	21	12	37	29
Moderate	44	48	41	48
Conservative	35	40	22	24
House vote				
Democratic	33	38	68	68
Republican	67	62	32	32

Source: 2006 National Exit Poll.

In order to determine whether long-term demographic changes were responsible for the generation gap in voting behavior, I compared the preferences of younger and older voters in the 2006 House elections while controlling for their demographic characteristics. The results displayed in Table 6.4 show that married white Christians younger than thirty were just as likely to vote for a Republican House candidate as married white Christians older than thirty. Similarly, voters older than thirty who were not married white Christians were just as likely to vote for a Democratic House candidate as voters younger than thirty who were not married white Christians. Thus, the current generation gap in voting behavior appears to be largely explained by the difference between the proportions of married white Christians in these two groups. The main reason that voters younger than thirty are now significantly more Democratic than older voters is that they are much less likely to be married, white, and Christian. This finding in turn suggests that the generation gap is not likely to disappear any time soon: today's younger generation of voters is likely to remain substantially more Democratic than its elders as it ages. Moreover, if future generations of voters have social characteristics similar to those of today's younger-than-thirty generation, there is a real potential for a major shift in party strength over the next few decades.

The Significance of Gender and Class

In addition to age, gender and class received a great deal of attention in connection with the 2008 presidential election. In particular, there was a great deal of speculation about Barack Obama's ability to appeal to two groups that formed the core of Hillary Clinton's electoral base in the Democratic primaries and whose support was widely considered to be critical to Democratic chances in the November election: white women and white working-class voters. A key assumption in much of this commentary was that class and gender play important roles in shaping voter preferences in the contemporary electorate. However, evidence from the 2004 and 2006 NEPs indicates that whether a voter is a married white Christian is a much stronger predictor of candidate preference than either gender or class.

Table 6.5 shows that whether an individual was a married white Christian had a much stronger influence on candidate choice in both the 2004 presidential election and the 2006 House elections than either gender or family income. In both elections, women who were married white Christians voted overwhelmingly for Republican candidates while men who were not married white Christians voted overwhelmingly for Democratic candidates. Thus, in 2004, 65 percent of female married white Christians and 71 percent of male married white Christians voted for George W. Bush, and 64 percent of females who were not married white Christians and 58 percent of males who were not married white Christians voted for John Kerry. Similarly, in 2006, 61 percent of female married white Christians and 64 percent of male married white Christians voted for a Republican House candidate, and 68 percent of females who were not married white Christians and 67 percent of males who were not married white Christians voted for a Democratic House candidate.

The results for class were very similar to those for gender: in both elec-

Table 6.5. Percentage voting Democratic in 2004 and 2006
by income and gender among married white Christians and others

	President, 2004		U.S. House, 2006	
	MWC	Others	MWC	Others
Gender				
Male	29	58	36	67
Female	35	64	39	68
Family income				
<30K	44	64	45	72
30–50K	32	61	36	70
50–75K	30	58	41	63
75–100K	31	66	39	63
100–150K	30	62	36	66
>150K	26	56	31	72

Source: 2004 and 2006 National Exit Polls.
Note: MWC indicates married white Christian.

tions lower income voters who were married white Christians overwhelmingly supported Republican candidates, and upper income voters who were
not married white Christians just as overwhelmingly supported Democratic
candidates. In 2004, 56 percent of voters with family incomes less than
$30,000 who were also married white Christians supported George Bush,
and 56 percent of voters with family incomes greater than $150,000 who
were not married white Christians supported John Kerry. The 2006 results
were even more striking: 55 percent of voters with family incomes less than
$30,000 who were also married white Christians voted for a Republican
House candidate, and 72 percent of voters with family incomes greater than
$150,000 who were not married white Christians voted for a Democratic
House candidate.

The proportion of married white Christians in the American electorate
has been declining for a long time. Moreover, the large generational difference in the prevalence of married white Christians in the contemporary elec-

torate suggests that this trend is likely to continue for the foreseeable future. What cannot be predicted as confidently is how party leaders will respond to this trend. Right now, Democrats appear likely to benefit from a continued decline in the proportion of married white Christians in the electorate because this group has strongly supported Republican candidates in recent elections whereas voters who are not married white Christians have strongly supported Democratic candidates.

Since the potential for additional Republican gains among married white Christians appears to be limited, Republican leaders will need to find ways to reduce the Democratic advantage among voters who are not married white Christians in order to maintain the party's competitive position. However, given the generally liberal views of this group, this will not be easy. Table 6.6 shows data from the 2004 ANES comparing the policy orientations of married white Christians with those of other voters on the eleven-item liberal-conservative issue scale. As described previously, this scale included questions on a wide variety of issues ranging from abortion and gay marriage to spending on social services and health insurance.

The results presented in the table indicate that voters who were not married white Christians held much more liberal views on the issues included in this scale than voters who were married white Christians. Almost 60 percent of voters who were married white Christians fell on the conservative side of the scale compared with less than 30 percent of voters who were not

Table 6.6. Policy orientations of married white Christians
and other voters in 2004

Policy orientation	MWC (%)	Others (%)
Liberal	24	49
Moderate	17	22
Conservative	59	29
Total	100	100
(n of cases)	(202)	(239)

Source: 2004 American National Election Study.
Note: MWC indicates married white Christian.

married white Christians. Moreover, the differences between these two groups of voters cut across all types of issues. Thus, 62 percent of voters who were not married white Christians took the prochoice position on the issue of abortion compared with 46 percent of voters who were married white Christians. Similarly, 54 percent of voters who were not married white Christians favored increased government spending on social services compared with 35 percent of voters who were married white Christians. Any attempt by Republican leaders to significantly increase their party's support among voters who are not married white Christians would therefore require changes in some of the party's longstanding policy commitments—changes that would clearly upset a large segment of the current Republican base.

Chapter Summary

Americans were more engaged in the 2008 presidential election than in any presidential election in the modern era, including the 2004 election, which set a recent record for voter turnout and for participation in campaign activities beyond voting. The interest and participation in the presidential campaign were driven in part by the prolonged and competitive contest between Barack Obama and Hillary Clinton for the Democratic nomination as well as enthusiasm among African Americans and young voters for Obama's candidacy, but the underlying reason for the high level of engagement among Democratic and Republican voters in 2008 was partisan-ideological polarization. With the Democratic and Republican presidential candidates taking sharply opposing positions on a wide range of domestic and international issues, and with Democrats almost certain to retain control of both houses of Congress with increased majorities, the stakes in the 2008 presidential contest were as high as they have been in any presidential election in recent history.

Beyond the short-term forces driving interest and participation in the 2008 presidential race, long-term societal trends are gradually altering the makeup of the American electorate. Since the 1950s, the proportion of college graduates in the electorate has more than tripled while the proportion of voters with a high school education or less has been cut in half. This rise in education levels has contributed to an increase in ideological sophistication in the electorate and, with it, an increase in partisan-ideological polarization. Voters who understand the meaning of ideological terms and concepts and the differences between the parties' ideological positions are much more likely to have consistent partisan and ideological preferences than voters who lack such understanding.

Along with the rise in education levels, changes in American society are also producing a more socially diverse electorate. Over the past fifty years, the proportion of nonwhite voters has increased from 6 percent to 26 percent; the proportion of non-Christians has increased from 6 percent to 18 percent; and the proportion of unmarried voters has increased from 14 percent to 41 percent. In the 1950s, almost 80 percent of voters were married white Christians; today, only a little over 40 percent of voters are married white Christians.

These trends have already had important effects on the composition of the Democratic and Republican electoral coalitions and the strategies of party leaders and candidates. Indeed, without these trends, Barack Obama would not have had a chance to win either the Democratic nomination or the presidential election. Today's Democratic coalition is a far cry from the Democratic coalition of the 1950s. Married white Christians have gone from 74 percent of Democratic voters in the 1950s to 29 percent of Democratic voters in the first decade of the twenty-first century. Among Democratic voters younger than thirty, a key Obama constituency, only 12 percent are married white Christians.

The ongoing transformation of the American electorate poses challenges for both major parties, but especially for Republicans because married white Christians make up a disproportionate share of their electoral base. The current generation gap in ideology and partisanship is largely a by-product of this transformation: because voters younger than thirty are much less likely to be married white Christians than older voters, they also have more liberal views and are more likely to identify with the Democratic Party than voters older than thirty. Their votes were a major factor in Democratic victories in the 2006 midterm election and in the 2008 presidential and congressional elections.

Unless these demographic trends reverse themselves, in order for the Republican Party to remain competitive in national elections, Republican strategists will have to find ways of expanding their party's support among the growing proportion of voters who are not married white Christians. Given the liberal policy preferences of this group, however, such an effort would require Republican candidates and elected officials to move their own positions closer to the center of the ideological spectrum—a move that would clearly risk alienating a large segment of the party's conservative base. And so far, at least, this is something that few Republican leaders have appeared willing to do.

7

Polarization and Representation

TODAY'S U.S. CONGRESS IS A very different body from the Congress of the
1960s and 1970s. One of the most important changes, because it has affected almost every aspect of the way Congress works, has been the rise of
partisan-ideological polarization. Over the past three decades, ideological
differences between Democrats and Republicans in the Senate and House
of Representatives have increased dramatically.[1] As recently as the 1970s,
both chambers had large numbers of moderate-to-conservative Democrats
and moderate-to-liberal Republicans. Moreover, conservative Democrats and
liberal Republicans held key leadership positions in the House and Senate,
serving as chairs or ranking minority members of major committees. Today,
however, there are very few moderates left in either party. The overwhelming majority of House and Senate Democrats are liberals, and the overwhelming majority of House and Senate Republicans are conservatives.
Conservative Democrats and liberal Republicans are virtually nonexistent
in both chambers. Certainly, no liberal Republicans or conservative Democrats serve as chairs or ranking minority members of major committees.[2]

Figure 7.1 illustrates the magnitude of the shift that has occurred in the
ideological makeup of the House of Representatives by comparing the ideological composition of the House during the 95th Congress (1977–1979)
with that during the 108th Congress (2003–2005). Members' ideological
positions were measured by their scores on the first dimension of the well-

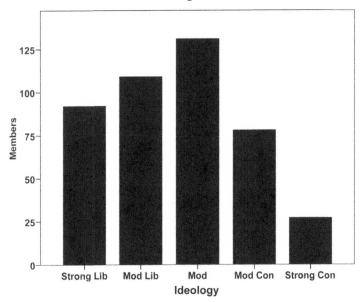

95th Congress

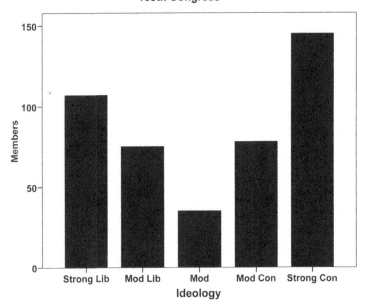

108th Congress

Table 7.1. Changing ideological composition of the congressional parties:
95th Congress versus 108th Congress

	95th Congress (%)	108th Congress (%)	Change (%)
Democrats			
Strong liberals	32	51	+19
Moderate liberals	37	36	−1
Moderates	29	13	−16
Conservatives	2	0	−2
Republicans			
Liberals	1	0	−1
Moderates	33	3	−30
Moderate conservatives	50	34	−16
Strong conservatives	16	63	+47

Source: "DW-NOMINATE Scores with Bootstrapped Standard Errors," updated 23 January 2009, http://voteview.com/dwnomin.htm.

known DW-NOMINATE scale developed by Keith Poole and Howard Rosenthal.[3] These scores were then collapsed into five categories.[4]

The contrast between the two distributions is striking. Between the 95th Congress and the 108th Congress, the moderate bloc shrank from 30 percent of the membership to only 8 percent. Meanwhile, strong conservatives grew from only 6 percent of the membership in the 95th Congress to 33 percent in the 108th Congress—by far the largest ideological bloc. Strong liberals and conservatives combined grew from 27 percent of House members in the 95th Congress to 57 percent of House members in the 108th Congress.

The dramatic increase in ideological polarization in the House of Representatives reflected fundamental changes in the ideological makeup of both

Figure 7.1. (Left) Ideologies of U.S. representatives in the 95th and 108th Congresses. (*Source:* "DW-NOMINATE Scores with Bootstrapped Standard Errors," http://voteview.com/dwnomin.htm.)

congressional parties, but especially in that of the Republican Party. Table 7.1 compares the ideological composition of the Democratic and Republican parties in the 95th and 108th Congresses. The data show that during this period House Democrats became somewhat more liberal while House Republicans became much more conservative. Strong liberals went from about a third of House Democrats in the 95th Congress to more than half of House Democrats in the 108th Congress; strong conservatives went from about a sixth of House Republicans in the 95th Congress to almost two-thirds of House Republicans in the 108th Congress. The question this raises, of course, is, what explains the growth of partisan-ideological polarization in the House of Representatives?

The Redistricting Hypothesis

Congressional scholars have described the growing ideological division between the congressional parties and examined its consequences for the legislative process.[5] There has been less research on the causes of increasing polarization in Congress.[6] Journalists and reform advocates, however, almost universally agree that the main cause of growing polarization in the House of Representatives is partisan redistricting.[7] In a recent article in *Governing Magazine,* Alan Greenblatt observed that "there's a growing consensus among good-government reformers that partisan mapmaking is the cause of many, if not most, contemporary political problems," including polarization.[8]

According to the redistricting hypothesis, state legislatures armed with computerized databases and sophisticated map-making programs have increasingly been drawing congressional districts that are safe for one party or the other.[9] Members elected from these safe districts have no need to take moderate positions to appeal to swing voters. They only need to cultivate their own party's primary voters, who tend to hold more extreme views than the overall electorate. The result is a House increasingly made up of liberal and conservative ideologues who have little interest in forging bipartisan coalitions or even in maintaining civility within the chamber.[10]

The redistricting hypothesis appears to enjoy nearly universal acceptance among journalists and reform advocates, but several recent studies by political scientists have raised questions about its validity. These studies have concluded that, contrary to the conventional wisdom, redistricting had little or nothing to do with the recent decline in competition in House elections. Other developments, such as the growing financial advantage of incumbents and increasing partisanship in the electorate, appear to be more responsible for the decline in competitive House races.[11]

Another major problem for the redistricting hypothesis is the fact that ideological polarization has been increasing in the Senate as well as in the House of Representatives even though state boundaries have not changed. As Keith Poole has observed, this clearly suggests that "the forces driving these changes in the party means over time are the same for both chambers."[12] Seeking to explain the growth of polarization in the Senate despite the absence of redistricting, Norman Ornstein and Barry McMillion argue that partisan gerrymandering indirectly affected the Senate because "a number of these sharp-edged representatives have . . . moved to the Senate, where they have helped widen the partisan gulf."[13] However, they present no evidence that former representatives are more ideologically extreme than other senators or that their presence has contributed to growing polarization in the upper chamber.

The redistricting hypothesis can be divided into two parts:

1. Partisan redistricting has caused an increase in the number of safe districts and a decrease in the number of marginal districts in the House of Representatives.
2. The decreasing competitiveness of House districts has caused an increase in polarization in the chamber.

This chapter tests these two parts by examining changes in the competitiveness of House districts between 1980 and 2002 and by analyzing the relationship between district competitiveness and ideological polarization in the 95th (1977–1979) and 108th (2003–2005) Congresses. Neither part of the redistricting hypothesis is supported.

The evidence indicates that partisan redistricting was not a major factor in the decline of marginal districts between 1980 and 2002 and that ideological polarization has increased among representatives from both marginal and safe districts. In the 108th Congress, representatives from marginal districts were almost as polarized as those from safe districts. Partisan redistricting can be criticized on other grounds, but it appears to have little or nothing to do with the rise of polarization in the House of Representatives. I conclude by proposing and testing an alternative explanation for increasing ideological polarization in Congress—one that can explain increasing polarization in the Senate as well as the House: increasing ideological polarization among Democratic and Republican voters.[14]

Changes in District Competitiveness

I use the normalized presidential vote to measure the partisan composition of House districts. The normalized presidential vote is simply the difference between the Democratic percentage of the major party vote in a House district and the Democratic percentage of the major party vote in the nation. Districts that are at least 10 points more Democratic than the nation are classified as safe Democratic; districts that are between 5 and 10 points more Democratic than the nation are classified as solid Democratic; districts that are between 5 points more Republican than the nation and 5 points more Democratic than the nation are classified as marginal; districts that are between 5 and 10 points more Republican than the nation are classified as solid Republican; and districts that are at least 10 points more Republican than the nation are classified as safe Republican.

This classification system does an excellent job of predicting the outcomes of House elections. In the 108th Congress, all 103 safe Democratic seats were held by Democrats, and 93 of 103 safe Republican seats were held by Republicans. Of the 116 seats classified as marginal, 72 were held by Republicans and 44 by Democrats.

The normalized presidential vote shows a substantial decline in the competitiveness of House districts since the 1970s. Table 7.2 compares the competitiveness of House districts in the 95th and 108th Congresses. The data show that the number of marginal districts fell from 187 (43 percent) in the 95th Congress to 116 (27 percent) in the 108th Congress while the number of safe districts rose from 122 (28 percent) in the 95th Congress to 203 (47 percent) in the 108th Congress. Both safe Democratic and safe Republican districts increased substantially—the number of safe Democratic districts increased from 71 to 103, and the number of safe Republican districts from 51 to 100.

Table 7.2. Competitiveness of House districts in the 95th and 108th Congresses

District type	95th Congress	108th Congress	Change
Safe Republican	51	100	+49
Solid Republican	77	72	−5
Marginal Republican	105	65	−40
Marginal Democratic	82	51	−31
Solid Democratic	49	44	−5
Safe Democratic	71	103	+32
Total safe	122	203	+81
Total solid	126	116	−10
Total marginal	187	116	−71

Source: Gary Jacobson and data compiled by author.
Note: Values shown are the number of districts.

As a result of these trends, the competitiveness of both parties' House districts changed dramatically. Table 7.3 compares changing characteristics of Democratic and Republican districts in the 95th and 108th Congresses. In this table, "high-risk districts" are districts that are at least 5 points more supportive of the opposing party than the nation. Historically, these districts have been the most likely to experience a change in party control. Since 1956, an average of 11 percent of seats held by incumbents in high-risk districts have switched parties compared with only 4 percent of seats held by incumbents in all other districts; over the same period, an average of 56 percent of open seats in high-risk districts have switched parties compared with only 28 percent of all other open seats.

Table 7.3 shows that between the 95th and 108th Congresses, the proportion of Democrats from safe districts rose from 24 percent to 49 percent while the proportion of Democrats from marginal and high-risk districts fell from 60 percent to 32 percent; during the same period, the proportion of Republicans from safe districts rose from 27 percent to 40 percent while the proportion of Republicans from marginal and high-risk districts fell from 46 percent to 34 percent.

Table 7.3. Changing characteristics of Democratic and Republican
constituencies: 95th Congress versus 108th Congress

	95th Congress (%)	108th Congress (%)	Change (%)
Democrats			
South	27	26	−1
North	73	74	+1
Safe districts	24	49	+25
Solid districts	16	19	+3
Marginal districts	43	21	−22
High-risk districts	17	11	−7
Republicans			
South	19	33	+14
North	81	67	−14
Safe districts	27	40	+13
Solid districts	27	26	−1
Marginal districts	43	31	−12
High-risk districts	3	3	0

Source: Gary Jacobson and data compiled by author.

Table 7.3 also shows that in addition to the increasing proportions of Democrats and Republicans from safe districts and the decreasing proportions from marginal and high-risk districts, the proportion of Republicans from the South increased substantially. The proportion of Democrats from the eleven states of the old Confederacy did not change much between the 95th and 108th Congresses, although the actual number of Democrats from these states declined considerably. Meanwhile, the number of Republicans from the South increased dramatically, and the proportion of House Republicans from the South rose from only 19 percent in the 95th Congress to 33 percent in the 108th Congress. Republicans were not only a much larger party in the 108th Congress; they were also a much more southern party, and since southern Republicans tend to be more conservative than their northern counterparts, this shift in the regional composition of the Republican Party could have contributed to the increasing conservatism of the entire House Republican delegation.

We have seen that, on the basis of presidential voting patterns, the competitiveness of House districts declined substantially between the 95th Congress and the 108th Congress. The question is to what extent redistricting was responsible for this decline. Figure 7.2 displays the trend between 1980 and 2002 in the numbers of safe and marginal seats in the House of Representatives before and after redistricting. The evidence indicates that although the number of safe districts increased considerably and the number of marginal districts decreased considerably, most of the change occurred between redistricting cycles. Only a small fraction of the decline in district competitiveness during this period appears to be a result of redistricting.[15]

But if redistricting was not responsible for the declining competitiveness of House districts, what was? The answer appears to be a combination of demographic change and party realignment. As a result of population move-

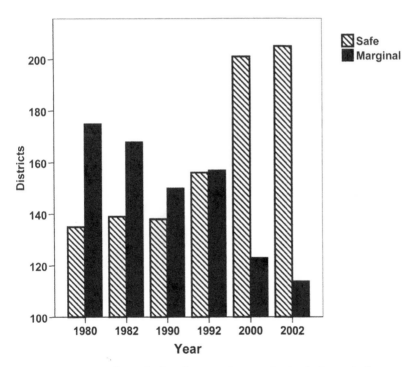

Figure 7.2. Numbers of safe and marginal House districts before and after redistricting, 1980–2002. (*Source:* Data compiled by Gary Jacobson and author.)

ment, immigration, and ideological realignment within the electorate, Republicans are increasingly surrounded by other Republicans and Democrats by other Democrats. Red states, counties, and congressional districts have been getting redder while blue states, counties, and congressional districts have been getting bluer.[16]

An examination of trends in presidential competition at the state level provides additional evidence that the declining competitiveness of House districts was a result of fundamental shifts in the geographical bases of partisanship rather than redistricting. Table 7.4 compares the results of the 1976 and 2004 presidential elections at the state level. Although the national margins of the winning candidates in these two elections were almost identical, the average winning margin at the state level was much greater in 2004 than in 1976: 14.8 percentage points versus 8.9 percentage points. There were far fewer competitive states and far more landslide states in 2004 than in 1976.

In 1976, the eight most populous states—California, Texas, New York, Illinois, Ohio, Pennsylvania, Michigan, and Florida—were all battlegrounds. The average margin of the winning presidential candidate in these states was 3.1 percentage points. In 2004, only four of these large states—Florida, Ohio,

Table 7.4. Declining competition in the states:
Comparison of the 1976 and 2004 presidential elections

	1976	2004
National vote margin	2.1%	2.5%
Average state margin	8.9%	14.8%
Number of states that were:		
Uncompetitive (10%+)	19	31
Competitive (0–5%)	24	12
Electoral votes of:		
Uncompetitive states	131	332
Competitive states	337	141

Source: Dave Leip's Atlas of U.S. Presidential Elections, http://www.uselectionatlas.org.

Pennsylvania, and Michigan—were battlegrounds. The remaining four—
California, Texas, New York, and Illinois—were won by margins ranging
from 10 to 23 percentage points. The average margin of the winning presidential candidate in the eight mega-states was 9.3 percentage points.

District Competitiveness and Polarization

The second part of the redistricting hypothesis states that the decreasing
competitiveness of House districts is responsible for the rise in ideological
polarization in the House of Representatives. Table 7.5 compares the ide-

Table 7.5. Average DW-NOMINATE scores of House Democrats and Republicans
in the 95th and 108th Congresses

	95th Congress	108th Congress	Change
All Democrats	−.29	−.40	−.11
All Republicans	.26	.46	+.20
Difference	.55	.86	+.31
Northern Democrats	−.35	−.44	−.09
Northern Republicans	.25	.44	+.19
Difference	.60	.88	+.28
Southern Democrats	−.13	−.29	−.16
Southern Republicans	.32	.51	+.19
Difference	.45	.80	+.25
Democrats from safe districts	−.36	−.49	−.13
Republicans from safe districts	.37	.53	+.16
Difference	.73	1.02	+.29
Democrats from marginal districts	−.28	−.34	−.06
Republicans from marginal districts	.22	.40	+.18
Difference	.50	.74	+.24

Source: "DW-NOMINATE Scores with Bootstrapped Standard Errors," updated 23 January 2009,
http://voteview.com/dwnomin.htm, Gary Jacobson, and data compiled by author.

ologies of Democrats and Republicans from safe and marginal districts in the 95th and 108th Congresses. This table also compares the ideologies of Democrats and Republicans from the North and South in these two Congresses to see whether the changing regional composition of the Republican Party contributed to growing ideological polarization.

Table 7.5 shows that ideological polarization increased substantially within every category of House members: northerners, southerners, those from safe districts, and those from marginal districts. Every Republican subgroup became more conservative, and every Democratic subgroup became more liberal, although the increases in conservatism among Republicans were generally larger than the increases in liberalism among Democrats. Since the increases in ideological polarization within each category were almost as large as the overall increase, it appears that neither the declining competitiveness of House districts nor the growing southern presence in the Republican Party explains more than a small fraction of the overall increase in ideological polarization between the 95th Congress and the 108th Congress.

Further evidence of the limited effect of district competitiveness on ideological polarization can be seen in Figure 7.3, which displays the relationship between the ideologies of Democrats and Republicans in the 108th Congress and the competitiveness of their districts. These results indicate that members representing marginal districts were only slightly less polarized than members representing districts dominated by supporters of their own party. Democrats representing marginal districts were almost as liberal as Democrats representing safe Democratic districts, and Republicans representing marginal districts were almost as conservative as Republicans representing safe Republican districts.

In order to more precisely estimate the contribution of district competitiveness to ideological polarization, I regressed the DW-NOMINATE scores of Democratic and Republican representatives in the 108th Congress on the partisan composition of their districts as measured by the normalized presidential vote. The intercept of the regression equation for each party provides a predicted DW-NOMINATE score for a member of that party from a politically neutral district—one that divided its vote evenly between Al Gore and George Bush in the 2000 presidential election.[17]

The regression analyses yielded predicted DW-NOMINATE scores of +.38

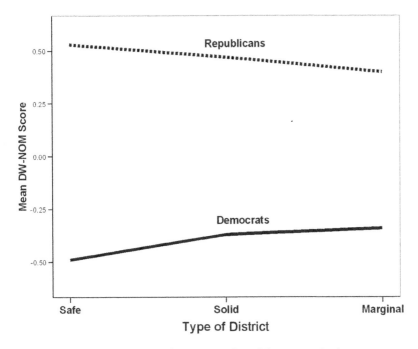

Figure 7.3. Ideological polarization in the 108th Congress by district competitiveness. (*Source:* "DW-NOMINATE Scores with Bootstrapped Standard Errors," http://voteview.com/dwnomin.htm and data compiled by author.)

for a Republican from a politically neutral district and −.31 for a Democrat from a politically neutral district. The difference between these two scores, .69, represents the predicted degree of ideological polarization of the congressional parties after the effects of district partisanship are removed. Comparing this difference with the overall difference of .86 between the Democratic and Republican means, we can estimate that district partisanship was responsible for only 20 percent of the overall level of ideological polarization in the 108th Congress.

The only House members in the 108th Congress who were substantially more moderate than their colleagues were those representing districts that normally favored the opposing party—Democrats from districts that were more Republican than the nation and Republicans from districts that were more Democratic than the nation. The average DW-NOMINATE score for

Democrats from Republican-leaning districts was −.21, compared with −.44 for all other Democrats. Similarly, the average DW-NOMINATE score for Republicans from Democratic-leaning districts was .31, compared with .48 for all other Republicans. However, both of these groups were much smaller in the 108th Congress than in the 95th Congress. In the 95th Congress, 39 percent of Democrats represented Republican-leaning districts, and 18 percent of Republicans represented Democratic-leaning districts. In contrast, in the 108th Congress, only 18 percent of Democrats represented Republican-leaning districts, and only 12 percent of Republicans represented Democratic-leaning districts.

The dramatic decline in the number of members representing districts that normally favor the opposing party was not caused by redistricting but by increased partisan voting in congressional elections. In the five elections between 1972 and 1980, the average correlation between the Democratic share of the normalized presidential vote and the Democratic share of the House vote was only .59. In the five elections between 1996 and 2004, the average correlation was .82. The proportion of variance in House election outcomes explained by district partisanship increased from 35 percent during the earlier time period to 67 percent during the later time period.

Because of this increase in partisan voting, it has become much more difficult for a Democratic or Republican candidate to win a seat in the House of Representatives from a district that normally favors the opposing party. Fewer Republicans now represent Democratic-leaning districts and far fewer Democrats now represent Republican-leaning districts. This means that compared with thirty years ago, far fewer members of Congress require significant support from the opposing party to win reelection. The large majority of members depend primarily on the votes of their own party's loyalists, and over the past three decades those party loyalists have become increasingly divided along ideological lines.

Partisan-Ideological Polarization in the Congressional Electorate

We can use data from the ANES to track ideological polarization in the American electorate since 1972. Figure 7.4 displays the trend between 1972

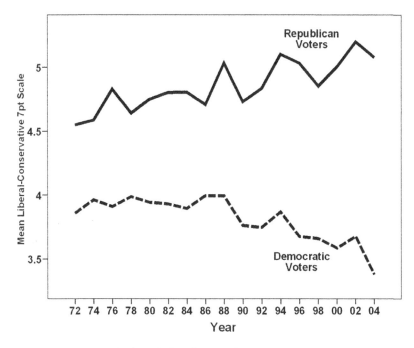

Figure 7.4. Average ideological identification of Democratic and Republican House voters, 1972–2004. (*Source:* American National Election Studies.)

and 2004 in the average scores of Democratic and Republican congressional voters on the 7-point liberal-conservative scale. These results demonstrate that ideological polarization among supporters of the two major parties has increased substantially—Democratic voters have been trending in a liberal direction while Republican voters have been trending in a conservative direction. The difference between the Democratic mean and the Republican mean more than doubled during these years—from 0.8 units in 1972 to 1.8 units in 2004.

Data from the 2004 NEP provide further evidence of ideological polarization in the congressional electorate. Table 7.6 compares the positions of Democratic and Republican congressional voters on a range of items included in the NEP survey: ideological identification, the role of the federal government, abortion, gay marriage, and the war in Iraq. On every one of these items, Democratic voters were much more liberal than Republican

Table 7.6. Ideological polarization in the 2004 congressional electorate:
Evidence from the National Exit Poll

Issue	Democratic voters	Republican voters	Difference
Ideological identification	62	25	37
Role of government`	67	31	36
Abortion	75	39	36
Gay marriage	56	31	25
Iraq and terrorism	72	14	58
Iraq and U.S. security	86	22	64
Average liberalism	70	27	43

Source: 2004 National Exit Poll.
Note: Entries represent percentage taking liberal position plus half of percentage taking moderate position.

voters, with the largest differences on the war in Iraq. Across these six items, the average liberalism score was 70 percent for Democratic voters and 27 percent for Republican voters.

Data from the 2004 ANES show that ideological polarization is fairly constant across different types of House districts. Figure 7.5 displays the average liberal-conservative score of Democratic and Republican voters in three types of House districts: strongly Republican, marginal, and strongly Democratic.[18] The results indicate that the ideologies of Democratic and Republican voters were very similar in all three types of districts. Democratic voters in strongly Republican and marginal districts were just as liberal as Democratic voters in strongly Democratic districts, and Republican voters in strongly Democratic and marginal districts were just as conservative as Republican voters in strongly Republican districts.

Data from the 2004 NEP provide additional evidence of ideological polarization among voters in all types of congressional districts. Table 7.7 compares the ideologies of Democratic and Republican voters in the 2004 NEP in strongly Republican districts, marginal districts, and strongly Democratic districts. Ideology here is measured by liberalism on six items: ideological

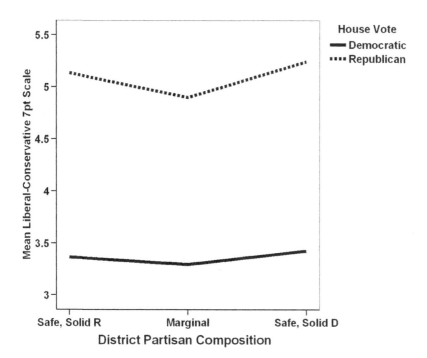

Figure 7.5. Ideologies of Democratic and Republican House voters in 2004
by district partisan composition. (*Source:* 2004 American National
Election Study and data compiled by author.)

Table 7.7. Ideological polarization in the 2004 congressional electorate:
Evidence from the National Exit Poll

	Type of House district		
	Safe, solid Republican	Marginal	Safe, solid Democrat
Democratic voters	67	72	71
Republican voters	26	30	29
Difference	41	42	42

Source: 2004 National Exit Poll.
Note: Entries represent average liberalism score (liberal percentage plus half of moderate per-
centage) on six items: ideological identification, role of government, abortion, gay marriage,
Iraq and national security, and Iraq and the war on terrorism.

identification, the role of the federal government, abortion, gay marriage, and two questions concerning the war in Iraq. The results again show that Democratic voters in strongly Republican and marginal districts were just as liberal as Democratic voters in strongly Democratic districts, and that Republican voters in strongly Democratic and marginal districts were just as conservative as Republican voters in strongly Republican districts.

Chapter Summary

Redistricting has been blamed for many of the current ills of American politics, including the lack of competition in elections, excessive partisanship, and ideological polarization in Congress. However, the evidence presented in this chapter indicates that redistricting had little or nothing to do with the rise of polarization in the House of Representatives. Instead, growing polarization in Congress appears to reflect growing polarization in the American electorate. Between the 95th and 108th Congresses, ideological polarization increased among House members from all types of districts—Democratic representatives from marginal and safe districts became more liberal, and Republican representatives from marginal and safe districts became more conservative. During the same period, ideological polarization among voters in congressional elections increased markedly—Democratic voters became more liberal, and Republican voters became more conservative.

In the 108th Congress, members representing marginal districts were almost as polarized as members representing safe districts: Democrats representing marginal districts were almost as liberal as Democrats representing safe Democratic districts, and Republicans representing marginal districts were almost as conservative as Republicans representing safe Republican districts. This appears to reflect the fact that the ideological beliefs of party supporters are very similar in marginal and safe districts: Democratic voters in marginal districts are as liberal as Democratic voters in safe Democratic districts, and Republican voters in marginal districts are as conservative as Republican voters in safe Republican districts.

Other factors, such as changes in voting rules and procedures and the growing influence of party leaders, may have contributed to the rise of ideological polarization in Congress.[19] However, the evidence presented in this chapter indicates that members of Congress generally reflect the views of their parties' electoral bases: Republicans reflect the views of their party's conservative electoral base, and Democrats reflect the views of their party's liberal electoral base. Polarization in Congress reflects polarization in the American electorate. Moreover, as I argue in the next chapter, growing partisan-ideological polarization has had profound consequences for the way Congress works and for the relationship between Congress and the president.

8

Polarization and Democratic Governance

AMERICAN POLITICS HAS CHANGED dramatically in the past half century. African Americans have secured the right to vote that was first guaranteed in the Fifteenth Amendment and now turn out at a rate equal to that of white Americans. Hispanics have grown from a tiny sliver of the electorate into a large and rapidly expanding voting bloc. Educational attainment has increased steadily. And the two-party system has undergone an ideological realignment. The Democratic and Republican parties today, although they remain broad-based coalitions, have much clearer ideological identities than in the past. Liberal Republicans and conservative Democrats, who once exercised considerable influence in their respective parties, have almost disappeared. Since the 1960s the ideological center of the Democratic Party has shifted to the left while the ideological center of the Republican Party has shifted to the right.

As a result of this ideological realignment, the electoral coalition forged by Franklin D. Roosevelt during the New Deal has disintegrated. Conservative southern whites, Catholics, and blue-collar voters have shifted their allegiance from the Democratic Party of their parents and grandparents to the Republican Party. At the same time, liberal whites and African Americans have moved more strongly into the Democratic camp. There is a much closer correspondence between party identification and ideology among the public, and especially among the politically engaged segment of the public —those who are politically interested, informed, and active. And because of increased consistency between policy preferences and partisanship, party loyalty in elections has reached its highest level in decades.

On the electoral side, the conditions for responsible party government in the United States have largely been met. The Democratic and Republican parties today offer voters a clear-cut choice between coherent policy packages, one liberal and one conservative, and most voters appear to have little difficulty choosing the party whose package is more to their liking. According to data from the ANES, the correlations between voters' ideological orientations and their party and candidate preferences are stronger today than at any time since the ANES began asking an ideological identification question in 1972.

Of course, not all Americans have a well-defined ideological orientation, and for those who do not, choosing between the liberal Democratic package and the conservative Republican package can be difficult. Some of these moderate or conflicted citizens may simply choose to opt out of the electoral process. Yet the overall level of engagement in the electoral process is as high as or higher than at any time in the past fifty years. Voter turnout, which increased substantially between 2000 and 2004, increased again between 2004 and 2008. Just as importantly, participation in activities beyond the act of voting has increased dramatically. According to the 2004 ANES, more than 40 percent of voting-age Americans tried to persuade a friend or neighbor to vote for their preferred candidate, easily the highest proportion in the history of the ANES, and more than 20 percent displayed a bumper sticker or yard sign, tying the all-time record set in 1960. A record 51 percent of ANES respondents reported engaging in at least one activity beyond voting in 2004, up from 37 percent in 2000. Participation was up in every demographic subgroup including eighteen-to-twenty-nine-year-olds, women, nonwhites, lower income Americans, and those with only a high school education.

Participation in the electoral process has been increasing because voters perceive more to be at stake in elections as a result of partisan-ideological polarization. With the Democratic and Republican presidential candidates presenting voters with a clear choice between sharply diverging sets of policies, the proportion of ANES respondents who perceived important differences between the parties and who indicated that they cared a great deal about the outcome of the presidential election both set all-time records in 2004. The increase in voter turnout and the extraordinary level of public engagement in the 2008 campaign suggest that public awareness of party differences and concern about the outcome of the presidential election may have been even higher in 2008.

But although the conditions for responsible party government have largely been met on the electoral side, with ideologically defined parties offering voters a clear choice between alternative sets of policies, the institutions of American government remain a major obstacle to effective party governance. The theory of responsible party government is based on a strongly majoritarian view of democracy.[1] This theory assumes that after an election is over, the winning party will carry out the will of the majority by implementing the policies on which it campaigned. However, many features of the American political system were deliberately designed to thwart the will of the majority. Divided party control of the legislative and executive branches, the presidential veto, the bicameral structure of the legislative branch, the overrepresentation of less populous states in the Senate, and the cloture rule in the Senate all have important antimajoritarian consequences.

Obstacles to Party Government

Divided Party Control

Divided party control of the executive and legislative branches, which is impossible in most parliamentary democracies, is a major obstacle to party governance in the United States. Because the president is elected separately from members of Congress, there is always a possibility of having one or both chambers of Congress and the White House controlled by different parties. In practice, however, divided party control was relatively rare during the first half of the twentieth century. Between 1900 and 1946, divided party control existed for only six of forty-six years. Since the end of World War II, however, divided party control has been much more common: between 1946 and 2008, at least one chamber of Congress and the presidency were controlled by different parties for thirty-eight of sixty-two years.[2]

From the standpoint of party responsibility, the problem with divided party government is that it makes it difficult, if not impossible, for voters to hold the governing party accountable for its policies and performance in office because there is not a single governing party. This was less of a problem during the first few decades after World War II because the policy differences between the parties were much smaller. With conservative Democrats and moderate Republicans exercising considerable influence, most major policy decisions were a product of bipartisan compromise. As a result, it made less difference which party controlled Congress or the presidency or whether different parties controlled the two branches. Policy outcomes under unified party control and divided party control were not very different. Today, however, policy differences between the parties are much greater, and bipartisan compromise is much more difficult. Divided party control is more likely to result in gridlock on major domestic issues and government by presidential fiat in the areas of national security and foreign policy.

The consequences of divided party control were clearly evident after Democrats regained control of the House and Senate in the 2006 midterm election. During the 2006 campaign, the Democratic leadership in Congress proposed an ambitious policy agenda, including an immediate increase in the minimum wage, reform of the Medicare prescription drug benefit, stronger environmental regulation, increased investment in mass transit and alternative energy, changes in labor law to facilitate union organizing, and, most prominently, rapid disengagement from Iraq. Two years later, other than an increase in the minimum wage, little of the Democratic agenda had been enacted into law.

Some of the problems during the 110th Congress were caused by divisions among congressional Democrats themselves. Increased Democratic numbers in the House and Senate also meant increased ideological diversity.[3] Many of the newly elected Democrats represented states and districts that had voted for George Bush in 2000 and 2004—districts that were considerably more conservative than the typical Democratic state or district. Not surprisingly, some of these newly elected Democrats were reluctant to support all of the items on the agenda proposed by the liberal leadership of their party, and with relatively narrow majorities, especially in the Senate, Democrats could not afford many defections from their own ranks.

But defections by moderate-to-conservative Democrats were not the biggest problem that Democratic leaders faced in the 110th Congress. Democrats were able to pass many of the key items on their agenda in the House of Representatives. The biggest problems that they ran into were an inability to muster the sixty votes needed to cut off a filibuster in the Senate and, of course, an inability to muster the votes needed to override a presidential veto. With only fifty-one Democrats in the Senate, including nominal Democrat Joseph Lieberman, Democratic leaders needed at least nine Republican votes to cut off debate on legislation. Given the relatively small number of moderate Republicans left in the Senate, getting nine Republican votes on any legislation opposed by the GOP leadership or President Bush proved to be very difficult. Needless to say, getting two-thirds majorities in both the House and Senate to override a presidential veto proved to be even more difficult. Congress did override presidential vetoes of broadly popular agricultural and water projects legislation and a bill raising reimbursement rates for doctors seeing Medicare patients. But when it came to any of the major items on the Democratic agenda, including setting a timetable for troop withdrawals from Iraq, little or nothing was accomplished during the 110th Congress. The result was growing frustration on the part of voters who thought that electing a Democratic Congress would result in major changes in government policy at home and abroad, frustration that undoubtedly contributed to the record low approval ratings that Congress received during 2008. According to the polls, it wasn't just Republicans who had a low opinion of the 110th Congress—even Democrats were dissatisfied with its performance.[4]

The 2008 elections gave Democrats control of the legislative and executive branches for the first time in fourteen years, but divided party control is likely to return at some point in the not too distant future for several reasons. The relatively close partisan division of the U.S. electorate means that neither Democrats nor Republicans are likely to dominate presidential or congressional elections for any extended period of time. Majorities in the House and Senate are likely to remain relatively slim, and switches in party control may be fairly common. Moreover, the uniquely American institution of midterm elections makes divided party control even more likely. No matter which party controls the White House, midterm elections generally result in gains for the opposition party, and in an era of narrow partisan majorities, those gains may frequently be large enough to result in a shift in party control of one or both chambers of Congress. Finally, a bicameral legislature increases the likelihood of divided party control because the opposition party only needs to gain a majority of seats in one of the two chambers. This occurred most recently during 2001–2003 after one Republican senator, James Jeffords of Vermont, decided to become an independent and join the Democratic caucus in the Senate. Jeffords's switch gave the Democrats fifty-one seats and control of the Senate until January 2003 while Republicans continued to control the House of Representatives.

The Senate

Divided party control may be the most obvious obstacle to responsible party government in the United States, but it is far from the only one. The Senate, with its antimajoritarian rules and overrepresentation of small states, is another potential roadblock to effective party governance. Of course the Senate, like the Electoral College, was deliberately designed by the framers of the Constitution to serve as a brake on the influence of shifting popular majorities. Not only was each state, regardless of population, given two seats in the upper chamber, but senators were originally chosen not by the voters but by the state legislatures. And with six-year terms and only one-third of its members up for reelection every other year, the Senate was also intended to be relatively insulated from the shifting tides of public opinion.

The Senate today is obviously a very different and more democratic institution than the body designed by the framers.[5] Since the ratification of the Seventeenth Amendment to the Constitution in 1913, members of the Senate have been elected directly by the people.[6] And in recent years Senate elections have actually been more competitive than House elections. But the Senate remains one of the most malapportioned legislative bodies in the world. With each state having two senators regardless of population, a senator from the least populous state, currently Wyoming, represents about half a million people while a senator from the most populous state, California, represents more than thirty-seven million people. Thus, a resident of Wyoming has more than seventy times as much influence in the U.S. Senate as a resident of California. Several counties in California have more residents than states such as Wyoming, Alaska, North Dakota, South Dakota, Vermont, and Montana.

The malapportionment of the Senate is politically significant because Democratic voters are concentrated disproportionately in the large metropolitan areas of the most populous states while Republicans dominate most of the small, sparsely populated states. Thus, in the 2000 presidential election Al Gore received about a half million more votes than George W. Bush but carried only twenty-one of the fifty states. Gore carried six of the nine most populous states, but lost fifteen of the twenty least populous states. The nine most populous states include more than half of the entire U.S. population but elect only 18 percent of the members of the Senate. Meanwhile, the twenty least populous states include less than 10 percent of the U.S. population but elect 40 percent of the members of the Senate. In the 110th Congress, Democrats held thirteen of the eighteen seats from the nine most populous states but only nineteen of the forty seats from the twenty least populous states. And the overrepresentation of sparsely populated states in the Senate is carried over into the Electoral College because a state's electoral votes are determined by its combined membership in the House and Senate. If electoral votes were based on House membership alone, Gore would have won the 2000 presidential election even without Florida.

The Senate's peculiar rules, and especially its tradition of requiring a supermajority vote to cut off debate, may represent an even greater obstacle to responsible party government than its severe malapportionment. In sharp contrast to the House of Representatives, where the time allocated for debate is strictly limited and the majority party has almost total control over the agenda, Senate rules allow unlimited time for debate unless cloture is invoked. This currently requires sixty votes. As a result, for most purposes a simple majority is not enough to pass a bill in the Senate. Most pieces of legislation must have the support of at least sixty members in order to pass.

Opponents of legislation can prevent action as long as they can muster at least forty-one votes in the Senate to block cloture. In the past, those opposed to a bill would actually have to hold the floor for hours or even days in order to prevent a vote. Today, however, actual filibusters are relatively rare. Opponents simply have to demonstrate that they have enough votes to block cloture, and the majority party leadership will generally pull a bill from the calendar in order to avoid tying up the floor and delaying other Senate business.

Beyond actually blocking legislation, the filibuster rule in the Senate can force changes in the content of legislation to satisfy the demands of members of the minority party. This was clearly the case with the economic stimulus legislation proposed by President Obama during his first weeks in office. In order to avert a Republican filibuster, the stimulus bill needed at least sixty votes in the Senate. Since there were only fifty-eight Democrats, at least two Republicans had to be persuaded to support the bill. The result was that three moderate Republican senators were able to force Senate Democrats to accommodate their preference for smaller spending increases and larger tax cuts than those in the House version of the bill.

Overcoming Gridlock

Bipartisan Compromise

Barring major constitutional reform, which appears highly unlikely in the foreseeable future, the antimajoritarian features of the American political system will remain important obstacles to effective party governance. This leaves two main approaches to overcoming the sort of partisan gridlock that has characterized American government since the 2006 midterm election and, indeed, for much of the past half century: bipartisan compromise and partisan dominance.

Bipartisan compromise is clearly the preferred route to overcoming gridlock among most mainstream commentators on American politics. Calls for bipartisanship in dealing with the major challenges facing American society, from social security and health care to immigration and national security, abound in the media. Moreover, a superficial reading of public opinion suggests that there is strong support for bipartisanship among the American people. According to recent polls, Americans believe that there is too much partisan bickering in Washington and want Democrats and Republicans to work together to find solutions to the country's problems.[7]

There are, of course, numerous examples of successful bipartisan compromise throughout American history, and even in relatively recent American history. For twenty years after the end of World War II, bipartisan compromise allowed the United States to pursue a policy of containment in dealing with the threat of the Soviet Union. It took the Vietnam War and the rise of a mass antiwar movement to disrupt the procontainment consensus in both parties. Even during the 1980s and 1990s, however, bipartisan coalitions of the center against the extremes were successful in passing major policy initiatives, including social security reform, welfare reform, and free trade agreements.[8]

In the past decade, however, and especially since the election of George W. Bush, there have been few examples of successful bipartisan compromise on major policy issues. During Bush's first term the one major policy initiative enacted with the support of a broad bipartisan coalition was the No Child Left Behind Act, which dramatically increased the role of the federal government in primary and secondary education. On other domestic issues, however, including tax cuts and social security, the president adopted a strongly partisan strategy, using the GOP's control of the House of Representatives to pass legislation, with little or no input from Democrats, while trying to peel away enough moderate Democrats in the Senate to prevent a filibuster. The strategy was successful on tax cuts but ultimately failed on social security reform because of Republican defections and resistance from moderate Democrats.

The failure of comprehensive immigration reform, the one major attempt at bipartisan policy-making during Bush's second term, clearly illustrates the limits of bipartisanship under conditions of intense partisan-ideological polarization. Despite the support of the Democratic leadership of the House and Senate and many prominent Republicans, including the party's eventual presidential candidate John McCain, the president's comprehensive reform package failed because of intense opposition from his own party's base to the bill's proposal of a "path to citizenship" for illegal aliens. Conservative talk show hosts and commentators fanned the flames of opposition to the president's proposal by attacking it as an "amnesty" bill. Forced to choose between supporting the president and offending many of their party's activists and voters, a majority of Republicans sided with their base.[9]

After the failure of immigration reform, Bush largely abandoned efforts at bipartisan compromise. Instead, he adopted a strategy of using recess appointments, executive orders, and administrative rule-making to implement his policies through the federal bureaucracy. With Democrats controlling both chambers of Congress, any major legislation proposed by the president would almost certainly have been viewed as dead on arrival on Capitol Hill in any event. During the last two years of his term, the principal objective of the president and the Republican leadership in Congress was to block Democratic legislative initiatives through the use of filibuster threats in the Senate and, when necessary, presidential vetoes. By the middle of 2008, however, Bush's dismal approval ratings in combination with the approaching elections had severely reduced his influence with congressional Republicans. Even the threat of a collapse of the nation's banking system could not stop a majority of House Republicans from voting against a Bush-backed $700 billion financial rescue bill in September 2008. The bill passed only because a majority of House Democrats supported it. Three months later, the administration's proposal to provide $14 billion in emergency financing to the nation's troubled automakers failed as a result of Republican opposition in the Senate.

It would be easy to blame George Bush for the failure of bipartisan coalition-building during most of his presidency, and especially during his second term. His confrontational approach to governing certainly made efforts at bipartisan cooperation more difficult than they might have been under a president with a different leadership style. But the failure of bipartisanship during the Bush years had much deeper roots. On the most fundamental level, the difficulty in building traditional bipartisan coalitions—coalitions of the center against the extremes—is that the center has largely disappeared in American politics. Not only are there few moderate Republicans and Democrats left in Congress, but the parties' electoral coalitions, and especially the politically engaged members of those coalitions, have moved farther and farther apart in their policy preferences and ideological positions over the past several decades. As a result, today, few members of Congress are willing to risk offending their most active and knowledgeable supporters by being seen consorting with the enemy. Even if Democrats and Republicans in Congress want to compromise, their ability to do so is severely constrained by the deep divisions that exist between politically engaged Democrats and Republicans.

At first glance it may seem strange that being perceived as practicing bipartisanship can be politically damaging. After all, polls show that many Americans dislike the excessive partisanship that has characterized American politics in recent years and favor bipartisan compromise. The problem, though, is that Democrats and Republicans, and especially politically engaged Democrats and Republicans, have very different ideas of what bipartisanship means. To politically engaged partisans, bipartisanship means that those on the opposing side should acknowledge the error of their ways and change their positions. These politically engaged partisans believe, in all sincerity, that those on the other side are wrong, if not immoral, and that therefore the solution to partisan gridlock is for those on the other side to simply surrender. Needless to say, this situation is not very conducive to real compromise, in which each side must give in to some of the demands of the other side.

Partisan Dominance

Although bipartisan compromise has at times been a successful strategy for addressing important national problems, dramatic changes in domestic policy generally occur during periods of partisan dominance—those relatively brief and infrequent interludes during which a party with a clear policy agenda dominates the political landscape. The most dramatic example of such a period in the past century was, of course, the New Deal. In the depths of the Great Depression and with Democrats enjoying overwhelming majorities in the both the House and Senate, Franklin D. Roosevelt was able to quickly push through Congress an ambitious set of legislative proposals that dramatically expanded the role of the federal government in American society.

Thirty years later, another Democratic president, Lyndon Johnson, took advantage of his enormous popularity in the wake of the assassination of President Kennedy and his landslide victory over Republican Barry Goldwater in the 1964 presidential election to push his Great Society legislation through a two-to-one Democratic House and Senate. Johnson's legislative program included Medicare—the most significant expansion of the federal government's role in American society since the New Deal—along with the War on Poverty and the most ambitious set of civil rights laws since the end of Reconstruction, including the landmark Voting Rights Act of 1965. All of Johnson's Great Society and civil rights legislation received considerable support from moderate Republicans, but it was the supermajorities of Democrats elected in 1964 that ensured there would be enough votes to overcome the coalition of conservative Republicans and southern Democrats that had dominated Congress for most of the 1950s and 1960s and that had successfully blocked civil rights and other liberal legislation.[10]

To a lesser extent, Ronald Reagan's defense buildup and cuts in taxes and domestic social programs during the early 1980s can also be seen as products of a period of partisan dominance in Washington. Reagan's decisive victory over Democratic incumbent Jimmy Carter in the 1980 presidential election, along with dramatic Republican gains in the House and Senate elections, gave Republicans effective control over the executive and legislative branches. Although Democrats still held a majority of seats in the House of Representatives, the first Republican majority in the Senate since the 1950s and an expanded coalition of conservative Republicans and southern Democrats in the House provided Reagan with enough votes to enact most of his major legislative proposals during his first two years in office.[11]

The Outlook for 2009 and Beyond

Despite the departure of George Bush and the arrival of a new team in the White House, partisan-ideological polarization is not going away any time soon. Barack Obama has received praise from prominent Republicans for some of his cabinet appointments, and he appears to be genuinely interested in working with Republican leaders in the House and Senate in developing legislation to deal with the nation's economic crisis. Obama is not the left-wing ideologue portrayed in Republican attack ads during the 2008 presidential campaign. Nevertheless, the prospects for bipartisan cooperation and compromise on major issues during Obama's presidential term are poor. Even if efforts at bipartisanship are sincere and not mere window dressing, the differences between the two parties on almost every major domestic and foreign policy issue are so great and the numbers of moderates in both parties are so small that reaching any agreement will be almost impossible. This became evident during Obama's first month in office when he sought to enlist the support of congressional Republicans for his economic stimulus program. Despite Obama's efforts, which included meeting with House and Senate Republicans and modifying his proposal to include larger tax breaks and smaller spending increases, not a single House Republican and only three Senate Republicans, barely enough to avert a filibuster, voted for the legislation.

The ability of Democrats and Republicans in Congress to compromise on major issues is also severely constrained by the views of politically engaged partisans in the public. Not only do politically engaged Democrats and Republicans hold diametrically opposing views on a wide range of issues, but they intensely dislike and mistrust the leaders of the opposing party. As a result, any serious attempts at compromise by party leaders would almost certainly produce a backlash among their most politically active and informed supporters. It was exactly this sort of backlash from the Republican base that was largely responsible for the failure of comprehensive immigration reform in 2006. Congressional Republicans who supported the president's proposal, regardless of their conservative credentials, were attacked by conservative talk show hosts and pundits as being RINOs (Republicans in name only) or worse. Facing intense criticism from their own supporters, several Republicans quickly backed away from their support for the bill. More recently, fear of a backlash from engaged partisans has severely impeded efforts at reaching bipartisan compromises on such issues as trade and energy.

Given the current level of partisan-ideological polarization among political elites and engaged partisans, successful efforts at bipartisan cooperation and compromise are unlikely. That leaves partisan dominance as the only viable means of overcoming gridlock in Washington. Partisan dominance, however, is difficult to achieve because it requires one party to control the presidency and both houses of Congress with enough votes in the Senate to invoke cloture if necessary. It also requires that the majority party have a clear agenda and a high enough level of ideological cohesion to enact its agenda into law.

The conditions for partisan dominance have been present for only a few relatively brief periods in the past century. Each of those periods—the New Deal era of the 1930s, Lyndon Johnson's Great Society in the mid-1960s, and the Reagan Revolution of the early 1980s—began with a decisive victory by one party's candidate in the presidential election accompanied by major gains in both houses of Congress. Whether such a period of partisan dominance is possible in today's highly polarized political environment is unclear. Barack Obama scored a decisive victory in the 2008 presidential election, winning 365 electoral votes and 53 percent of the popular vote. He carried twenty-eight states, including thirteen of the fifteen most populous states, and his 9.5 million vote margin over John McCain was the largest for any presidential candidate since Reagan in 1984. Democrats also gained eight seats in the Senate and twenty-one seats in the House of Representatives, to give them their largest majorities in both chambers since 1995.

With his party firmly in control of Congress and the nation facing its most severe economic crisis in decades, it is clear that President Obama intends to dramatically change the nation's direction by reshaping the executive branch and moving an ambitious legislative agenda through Congress during his first two years in office. Given the high level of cohesion of the congressional parties today, the most important potential obstacle to effective Democratic control is the ability of Republicans to block the president's legislative agenda by filibustering or threatening to filibuster in the Senate.

Barack Obama was elected on a promise of bringing change to Washington. But during the campaign he talked about two kinds of change: change in the content of public policy, and change in the way Washington works and especially in what he described as the excessive partisanship of the Bush era. The problem is that these two kinds of change may be incompatible. Appointing a few Republicans to the cabinet, meeting with House and Senate Republicans at the Capitol, and inviting some Republican members of Congress to the White House may win Obama some compliments, but it is unlikely to win him any votes on legislation. That would require his making significant concessions on the content of any legislation.

The last two elections have drastically reduced the number of moderate Republicans in the House and Senate, leaving the party more dominated than ever by hard-line conservatives who represent safe Republican districts and states. In order to win more than token support from congressional Republicans, therefore, President Obama would have to make major policy concessions to these hard-line conservatives—concessions that would almost certainly be unacceptable not only to the vast majority of congressional

Change and Continuity in the 2004 and 2006 Elections (Washington, DC: CQ Press, 2007), chapter 11. For evidence concerning political engagement in 2008, see Frank Newport, "Democrats' Election Enthusiasm Far Outweighs Republicans'," Gallup Poll, http://www.gallup.com/poll/111115/Democrats-Election-Enthusiasm-Far-Outweighs-Republicans.aspx.

7. The most famous statement of the case for responsible party government in the United States and the conditions required to bring it about can be found in the report of the Committee on Political Parties of the American Political Science Association chaired by E. E. Schattschneider, "Toward a More Responsible Two-Party System," *American Political Science Review* 44, Supplement (1950). For a critique of the report and an examination of the difficulty of implementing responsible party government in the United States, see Austin Ranney, "Toward a More Responsible Two-Party System: A Commentary," *American Political Science Review* 45 (1951), pp. 488–499.

8. See for example Carl Hulse, "Off for Break, Congress May Still Face Stalemate," *New York Times*, November 17, 2007, p. 15.

9. Earl Black and Merle Black, *Divided America: The Ferocious Power Struggle in American Politics* (New York: Simon and Schuster, 2007).

10. Brownstein, *The Second Civil War*, chapter 6; Bill Bishop, *The Great Sort: Why the Clustering of Like-Minded America Is Tearing Us Apart* (New York: Houghton Mifflin, 2008).

11. See Frank Newport, "Americans Tuned in to the Election This Year," Gallup Poll, http://www.gallup.com/poll/103792/Americans-Tuned-Election-Year.aspx.

12. Jeffrey M. Jones, "Democrats Top Republicans on Election Enthusiasm," Gallup Poll, http://www.gallup.com/poll/103858/Democrats-More-Enthusiastic-Than-Republicans-About-Election.aspx.

Chapter 2. The Engaged Public

1. The classic statement of this position is found in Walter Lippmann, *Public Opinion* (New York: Harcourt, Brace, 1922). For a more recent overview of the literature on voter ignorance and apathy, see Ilya Somin, "Voter Ignorance and the Democratic Ideal," *Critical Review* 12 (1998), pp. 413–458.

2. Philip E. Converse, "The Nature of Belief Systems in Mass Publics," in David Apter, ed., *Ideology and Discontent* (New York: Free Press, 1964).

3. Morris P. Fiorina, with Samuel J. Abrams and Jeremy C. Pope, *Culture War? The Myth of a Polarized America* (New York: Pearson Longman, 2006), p. 19.

4. See Frank Newport, "Americans Tuned in to the Election This Year," Gallup Poll, http://www.gallup.com/poll/103792/Americans-Tuned-Election-Year.aspx.

5. For analyses of voter turnout in the United States, see Angus Campbell, Warren E. Miller, Donald E. Stokes, and Philip E. Converse, *The American Voter* (New York: John Wiley and Sons, 1960), chapter 5; Raymond E. Wolfinger and Steven J. Rosenstone, *Who Votes?* (New Haven, CT: Yale University Press, 1980); Ruy A. Teixeira, *The Disappearing American Voter* (Washington, DC: Brookings

Institution, 1992); Thomas E. Patterson, *The Vanishing Voter: Public Involvement in an Age of Uncertainty* (New York: Knopf, 2002); Warren E. Miller and J. Merrill Shanks, *The New American Voter* (Cambridge, MA: Harvard University Press, 1996), pp. 95–114; Michael P. McDonald and Samuel L. Popkin, "The Myth of the Vanishing Voter," *American Political Science Review* 95 (December 2001), pp. 963–974; Steven J. Rosenstone and John Mark Hansen, *Mobilization, Participation, and Democracy in America* (New York: Macmillan, 1993).

6. The classic statement of this theory is found in Anthony Downs, *An Economic Theory of Democracy* (New York: Harper and Row, 1957), chapter 14. See also John H. Aldrich, "Rational Choice and Turnout," *American Journal of Political Science* 37 (1993), pp. 246–278.

7. Wolfinger and Rosenstone, *Who Votes?*, chapters 2–3.

8. For additional evidence of the extraordinary degree of polarization in Americans' opinions about President Bush, see Gary C. Jacobson, *A Divider, Not a Uniter: The American People and George W. Bush* (New York: Pearson Longman 2007).

9. See, for example, Downs, *An Economic Theory.*

10. See Alan I. Abramowitz and Kyle L. Saunders, "Ideological Realignment in the U.S. Electorate," *Journal of Politics* 60 (1998), pp. 634–652.

11. See Alan I. Abramowitz and Walter J. Stone, "The Bush Effect: Polarization, Turnout, and Activism in the 2004 Presidential Election," *Presidential Studies Quarterly* 36 (2006), pp. 141–154.

12. For a thorough analysis of the Perot phenomenon, see Ronald B. Rapoport and Walter J. Stone, *Three's a Crowd: The Dynamics of Third Parties, Ross Perot, and Republican Resurgence* (Ann Arbor: University of Michigan Press, 2005).

13. See ibid., chapters 8–10.

14. Polls in the fall of 2008 indicated that none of the third-party or independent candidates—Libertarian Bob Barr, independent Ralph Nader, and Green Party nominee Cynthia McKinney—was attracting significant support. See Frank Newport, "Voters Not Clamoring for Third-Party Candidacy This Year," Gallup Poll, January 22, 2008, http://www.gallup.com/poll/103846/Voters-Clamoring-ThirdParty-Candidacy-Year.aspx.

Chapter 3. Partisan-Ideological Polarization

1. Philip E. Converse, "The Nature of Belief Systems in Mass Publics," in David Apter, ed., *Ideology and Discontent* (New York: Free Press, 1964).

2. Christopher H. Achen, "Mass Political Attitudes and the Survey Response," *American Political Science Review* 69 (1975), pp. 1218–1231.

3. Norman H. Nie and Kristi Anderson, "Mass Belief Systems Revisited: Political Change and Attitude Structure," *Journal of Politics* 36 (1974), pp. 540–591; Norman H. Nie and James N. Rabjohn, "Revisiting Mass Belief Systems Revisited: Or, Doing Research Is Like Watching a Tennis Match," *American Journal of Political Science* 23 (1979), pp. 139–175; James A. Stimson, "Belief Systems: Con-

straint, Complexity, and the 1972 Election," *American Journal of Political Science* 19 (1975), pp. 393–417.

4. George F. Bishop, Robert W. Oldenick, Alfred J. Tuchfarber, and Stephen E. Bennett, "The Changing Structure of Mass Belief Systems: Fact or Artifact," *Journal of Politics* 40 (1978), pp. 781–787; John L. Sullivan, James E. Piereson, George E. Marcus, and Stanley Feldman, "The More Things Change, the More They Stay the Same: The Stability of Mass Belief Systems," *American Journal of Political Science* 23 (1979), pp. 176–186.

5. Philip E. Converse, "Democratic Theory and Electoral Reality," *Critical Review* 18 (2006), pp. 297–329.

6. Keith T. Poole and Howard Rosenthal, *Congress: A Political-Economic History of Roll Call Voting* (New York: Oxford University Press, 1997); Poole and Rosenthal, "D-Nominate After 10 Years: A Comparative Update to Congress: A Political-Economic History of Roll-Call Voting," *Legislative Studies Quarterly* 26 (2001), pp. 5–29; Jeffrey M. Stonecash, Mark D. Brewer, and Mack D. Mariani, *Diverging Parties: Social Change, Realignment, and Party Polarization* (Boulder, CO: Westview, 2003); Ronald Brownstein, *The Second Civil War: How Extreme Partisanship Has Paralyzed Washington and Polarized America* (New York: Penguin, 2007).

7. Alan I. Abramowitz and Kyle L. Saunders, "Ideological Realignment in the U.S. Electorate," *Journal of Politics* 60 (1998), pp. 634–652; Marc J. Hetherington, "Resurgent Mass Partisanship: The Role of Elite Polarization," *American Political Science Review* 95 (2001), pp. 619–631; Geoffrey C. Layman and Thomas M. Carsey, "Party Polarization and 'Conflict Extension' in the American Electorate," *American Journal of Political Science* 46 (2002), pp. 786–802.

8. Morris P. Fiorina, with Samuel J. Abrams and Jeremy C. Pope, *Culture War? The Myth of a Polarized America* (New York: Pearson Longman, 2006), p. 19.

9. Donald R. Kinder, "Belief Systems Today," *Critical Review* 18 (Winter 2006), pp. 197–216.

10. Interest is measured by a single question asking about interest in the presidential campaign. Knowledge is measured by ten items including questions about party control of the House and Senate, the jobs held by various political leaders, and ability to accurately place the presidential candidates on a liberal-conservative ideology scale and an abortion policy scale. Participation is measured by six items asking about participation in campaign-related activities including voting, trying to influence the vote of a friend or relative, displaying a bumper sticker or yard sign, contributing money to a party or candidate, attending a campaign meeting or rally, and working on a campaign.

11. For a detailed explanation of the sampling procedure used in this survey, see Douglas Rivers, "Sample Matching: Representative Sampling from Internet Panels," unpublished paper available at http://www.polimetrix.com.

12. Bruce E. Keith, David B. Magleby, Candice J. Nelson, Elizabeth Orr, Mark Westlye, and Raymond W. Wolfinger, *The Myth of the Independent Voter* (Berkeley: University of California Press, 1992).

13. The wording of the questions included in the CCES survey can be found on the Cooperative Congressional Election Study website, "2006 Common Content Page," at http://web.mit.edu/polisci/portl/cces/commoncontent.html.

14. Converse, "The Nature of Belief Systems."

15. Poole and Rosenthal, *Congress.*

16. Larry M. Bartels, "Partisanship and Voting Behavior, 1972–1996," *American Journal of Political Science* 44 (2000), pp. 35–50.

17. Keith et al., *The Myth of the Independent Voter.*

18. Donald Green, Bradley Palmquist, and Eric Schickler, *Partisan Hearts and Minds: Political Parties and the Social Identities of Voters* (New Haven, CT: Yale University Press, 2002); Alan I. Abramowitz and Kyle L. Saunders, "Exploring the Bases of Partisanship in the American Electorate: Social Identity vs. Ideology," *Political Research Quarterly* 59 (2006), pp. 175–188.

Chapter 4. Polarization and Social Groups

1. Results of presidential, congressional, and gubernatorial elections during this period can be found in *Congressional Quarterly's Guide to U.S. Elections*, 5th ed. (Washington, DC: CQ Press, 2005).

2. See Angus Campbell, Philip E. Converse, Warren E. Miller, and Donald E. Stokes, *The American Voter* (New York: John Wiley and Sons, 1960), chapter 10.

3. For an analysis of the sources of support for Roosevelt, see Edgar E. Robinson, *They Voted for Roosevelt: The Presidential Vote, 1932–1944.* The social bases of the vote in the 1944 presidential election in one Ohio city are examined in Paul F. Lazarsfeld, Bernard Berelson, and Hazel Gaudet, *The People's Choice: How the Voter Makes Up His Mind in a Presidential Campaign* (New York: Columbia University Press, 1948). An analysis of the party coalitions in one upstate New York county in the 1948 presidential election can be found in Bernard R. Berelson, Paul F. Lazarsfeld, and William N. McPhee, *Voting: A Study of Opinion Formation in a Presidential Campaign* (Chicago: University of Chicago Press), chapter 4.

4. On the battle for black voting rights and the effects of the 1965 Voting Rights Act, see Alexander Keyssar, *The Right to Vote: The Contested History of Democracy in the United States* (New York: Basic Books, 2000), chapter 8. See also Clarence Lusane, *No Easy Victories: Black Americans and the Vote* (New York: Franklin Watts, 1996).

5. Campbell et al., *American Voter*, chapter 10.

6. See V. O. Key Jr., *Southern Politics in State and Nation* (New York: Alfred A. Knopf, 1949).

7. See Nathan Glazer and Daniel Patrick Moynihan, *Beyond the Melting Pot: The Negroes, Puerto Ricans, Jews, Italians, and Irish of New York City* (Cambridge, MA: M.I.T. Press, 1963), for an in-depth examination of the process of cultural and political integration of immigrants in America's largest city. For an analysis of the effect of immigration on American political and cultural history, see Oscar Handlin, *Immigration as a Factor in American History* (Englewood Cliffs, NJ:

6. For an excellent analysis of the shift of conservative politicians in the South from the Democratic Party to the Republican Party over the past several decades, see Earl Black and Merle Black, *The Rise of Southern Republicans* (Cambridge, MA: Harvard University Press, 2002). The decline of moderate-to-liberal Republicans outside of the South is chronicled in Brownstein, *The Second Civil War*, chapter 4. See also Nicol C. Rae, *The Decline and Fall of the Liberal Republicans from 1952 to the Present* (New York: Oxford University Press, 1989).

7. See Campbell et al., *The American Voter*, chapter 6. For a more recent discussion of the changing distribution of party identification in the American electorate, see Alan Abramowitz, *Voice of the People: Elections and Voting in the United States* (New York: McGraw Hill, 2004), chapter 3.

8. For additional evidence concerning the importance of partisan-ideological consistency for voter decision making, see D. Sunshine Hillygus and Simon Jackman, "Voter Decision Making in Election 2000: Campaign Effects, Partisan Activation, and the Clinton Legacy," *American Journal of Political Science* 47 (2003), pp. 583–596.

9. See Black and Black, *The Rise of Southern Republicans*.

10. For an in-depth examination of diverging trends in support of the parties across major regions of the country, including the growing dominance of the Democratic Party in the Northeast, see Earl Black and Merle Black, *Divided America: The Ferocious Power Struggle in American Politics* (New York: Simon and Schuster, 2007).

11. For evidence concerning these trends, see Alan I. Abramowitz, Brad Alexander, and Matthew Gunning, "Incumbency, Redistricting, and the Decline of Competition in U.S. House Elections," *Journal of Politics* 68 (2006), pp. 75–88. See also Abramowitz, Alexander, and Gunning, "Don't Blame Redistricting for Uncompetitive Elections," *PS: Political Science and Politics* 40 (2006), pp. 87–90.

12. See, for example, Judith Eilperin, *Fight Club: How Partisanship Is Poisoning the House of Representatives* (Lanham, MD: Rowman and Littlefield, 2006); Mark Monmonier, *Bushmanders and Bullwinkles: How Politicians Manipulate Electronic Maps and Census Data to Win Elections* (Chicago: University of Chicago Press, 2001); and Michael McDonald, "Drawing the Line on District Competition," *PS: Political Science and Politics* 40 (2006), pp. 91–94.

13. See, for example, David Broder, "No Vote Necessary," *Washington Post*, November 11, 2004, p. A-37.

14. For evidence concerning this trend, see Bruce I. Oppenheimer, "Deep Red and Blue Congressional Districts," in Lawrence C. Dodd and Bruce I. Oppenheimer, eds., *Congress Reconsidered*, 8th ed. (Washington, DC: Congressional Quarterly Press, 2005). See also Bill Bishop, *The Big Sort: Why the Clustering of Like-Minded America Is Tearing Us Apart* (New York: Houghton Mifflin, 2008).

15. For evidence of this trend, see Larry M. Bartels, "Partisanship and Voting Behavior, 1952–1996," *American Journal of Political Science* 44 (2000), pp. 35–50.

16. See Marjorie R. Hershey, *The Making of Campaign Strategy* (Lexington, MA: Lex-

ington Books, 1974). See also Paul S. Herrnson, *Congressional Elections: Campaigning at Home and in Washington*, 5th ed. (Washington, DC: Congressional Quarterly Press, 2007), chapter 7.

17. For evidence of this, see Thomas M. Holbrook and Scott D. McClurg, "The Mobilization of Core Supporters: Campaigns, Turnout, and Electoral Competition in United States Presidential Elections," *American Journal of Political Science* 49 (2005), pp. 689–703.

18. Green is the coauthor of what is generally considered the definitive study of the relative effectiveness of different techniques for increasing voter turnout. See Donald P. Green and Alan S. Gerber, *Get Out the Vote: How to Increase Voter Turnout* (Washington, DC: Brookings Institution Press, 2004).

19. Jonathan Tilove, "Cutting Edge Mobilization May Have Won the Day for Bush," *Newhouse News Service*, November 24, 2004.

20. See ibid. For a more skeptical analysis of the effectiveness of the GOP's 72-hour program, see Mark Mellman "72 Hours to Victory: Maybe Not," thehill.com, November 1, 2006, http://thehill.com/mark-mellman/72-hours-to-victory-maybe -not-2006–11–01.html.

21. Data on voter turnout in recent presidential elections can be found at McDonald's website, United States Election Project, "Voter Turnout": http://elections .gmu.edu/voter_turnout.htm.

22. The spending data are summarized in a table, "Presidential General Election Financing as of October 15, 2008," at the Campaign Finance Institute website: http://www.cfinst.org/president/pdf/Pres08_12G_Table1.pdf.

23. See FiveThirtyEight, "Obama Leads Better than 3:1 in Field Offices," http: //www.fivethirtyeight.com/2008/08/obama-leads-better-than-31-in-field.html.

24. See FiveThirtyEight, "The Contact Gap: Proof of the Importance of the Ground Game?" at http://www.fivethirtyeight.com/2008/11/contact-gap-proof -of-importance-of.html. The data can also be found in state exit poll results, "Exit Polls," available on the CNN website at http://www.cnn.com/ELECTION /2008/results/polls.main/.

25. Holbrook and McClurg, "The Mobilization of Core Supporters."

26. Stephen Ansolabehere, John Mark Hansen, Shigeo Hirano, and James M. Snyder Jr., "The Decline of Competition in U.S. Primary Elections, 1908–2004," unpublished manuscript, Department of Political Science, Massachusetts Institute of Technology, 2005.

27. The classic study of intraparty factionalism and primary competition at the state level is V. O. Key Jr., *Southern Politics in State and Nation* (New York: Alfred A. Knopf, 1949).

28. See Ron Klain, "A Fight about What?" *New York Times*, online edition, February 11, 2008, at http://campaignstops.blogs.nytimes.com/2008/02/11/a-fight -about-what.

29. See John B. Judis and Ruy Teixeira, *The Emerging Democratic Majority* (New York: Scribner, 2002).

88; Abramowitz, Alexander, and Gunning, "Don't Blame Redistricting for Uncompetitive Elections," *PS: Political Science and Politics* 40 (2006), pp. 87–90; John N. Friedman and Richard T. Holden, "The Rising Incumbent Reelection Rate: What's Redistricting Got to Do with It?," unpublished manuscript, Department of Economics, Harvard University.

12. Keith T. Poole, "The Decline and Rise of Party Polarization in Congress during the Twentieth Century," *Extensions*, Fall 2005, p. 8.

13. Norman Ornstein and Barry McMillion, "One Nation, Divisible," *New York Times*, June 24, 2005, p. A-23.

14. For a similar argument, see Gary C. Jacobson, "Partisan Polarization in Presidential Support: The Electoral Connection," *Congress and the Presidency* 30 (2003), pp. 1–36.

15. Abramowitz et al., "Incumbency, Redistricting."

16. See Bill Bishop, *The Big Sort: Why the Clustering of Like-Minded America Is Tearing Us Apart* (New York: Houghton Mifflin, 2008). See also Bruce I. Oppenheimer, "Deep Red and Blue Congressional Districts: The Causes and Consequences of Declining Party Competitiveness," in Dodd and Oppenheimer, eds., *Congress Reconsidered.*

17. The estimated equation for Republicans was DWNOM = .381 + .009 × PVDIFF. The estimated equation for Democrats was DWNOM = −.311 + .008 × PVDIFF. DWNOM represents the predicted score on the DW-NOMINATE scale, and PVDIFF represents the difference between the district share of the major party vote for the presidential candidate from the House incumbent's party and the national share of the major party vote for the presidential candidate from the House incumbent's party.

18. House districts included in the 2004 ANES and NEP were classified on the basis of the results of the 2004 presidential election. Districts that were at least 5 percentage points more Republican than the nation were classified as strongly Republican; districts that were at least 5 percentage points more Democratic than the nation were classified as strongly Democratic; and districts that were within 5 percentage points of the national party vote were classified as marginal.

19. See Theriault, "The Case of the Vanishing Moderates," and Theriault, "An Integrated Explanation."

Chapter 8. Polarization and Democratic Governance

1. The case for responsible party government in the United States was laid out in "Toward a More Responsible Two-Party System: A Report of the Committee on Political Parties," *American Political Science Review* 44 (1950), No. 3, Part 2, Supplement. Since then, the report has been the subject of numerous critiques that have questioned both the benefits of responsible party government and its feasibility in the American political context. Some of the most prominent of these include Austin Ranney, "Toward a More Responsible Two-

Party System: A Commentary," *American Political Science Review* 45 (1951), pp. 488–499; J. Roland Pennock, "Responsiveness, Responsibility, and Majority Rule," *American Political Science Review* 46 (1952), pp. 790–807; Evron M. Kirkpatrick, "Toward a More Responsible Two-Party System: Political Science, Policy Science, or Pseudo-Science?," *American Political Science Review* 65 (1971), pp. 965–990; Gerald M. Pomper, "Toward a More Responsible Two-Party System? What, Again?," *Journal of Politics* 33 (1971), pp. 916–940; Paul S. Herrnson, "Why the United States Does Not Have Responsible Parties," *Perspectives on Political Science* 21 (1992), pp. 91–98; and John Kenneth White, "Responsible Party Government in America," *Perspectives on Political Science* 21 (1992), pp. 80–90. All of these critiques, however, preceded the dramatic increase in partisan-ideological polarization among party elites and voters of the past few decades.

2. For an assessment of the consequences of divided party control for the policy-making process, see David. R. Mayhew, *Divided We Govern: Party Control, Lawmaking, and Investigations, 1946–1990* (New Haven, CT: Yale University Press, 1991). However, Mayhew's conclusion that divided party control has not had a major effect on policy outcomes may be limited to the time period covered by his study, which was one in which bipartisan cooperation and compromise were much more feasible than today. For a critique of Mayhew's findings, see Sarah A. Binder, "The Dynamics of Legislative Gridlock, 1947–96," *American Political Science Review* 93 (1999), pp. 519–533.

3. See Carl Hulse, "Gaining Seats, Democrats Find Their House Ideologically Divided," *New York Times*, May 18, 2008, p. 25.

4. See Lydia Saad, "Congress' Approval Rating Ties Lowest in Gallup Records," Gallup Poll, May 14, 2008, http://www.gallup.com/poll/107242/Congress -Approval-Rating-Ties-Lowest-Gallup-Records.aspx.

5. For a collection of essays on the role of the Senate in the contemporary American political system, see Bruce I. Oppenheimer, ed., *U.S. Senate Exceptionalism* (Columbus: Ohio State University Press, 2002).

6. Even before ratification of the Seventeenth Amendment, a number of states had enacted laws providing for popular election of U.S. senators. See U.S. Senate, "Direct Election of Senators," http://www.senate.gov/artandhistory/history /common/briefing/Direct_Election_Senators.htm.

7. See, for example, Jeffrey M. Jones, "Perceived Inaction Largely behind Low Ratings of Congress," Gallup Poll, September 5, 2007, http://www.gallup.com/poll /28600/Perceived-Inaction-Largely-Behind-Low-Ratings-Congress.aspx.

8. See Ronald Brownstein, *The Second Civil War: How Extreme Partisanship Has Paralyzed Washington and Polarized America* (New York: Penguin, 2007), especially chapters 3–4.

9. For a description of these developments, see Jonathan Weisman, "Senators Unmoved by Bush Bid to Save Immigration Bill," *Washington Post*, June 13, 2007, p. A-3.